QUICK PREP

Preparing for a
Child Custody Trial
What You Need to Know

Stan R. Weller

Project Manager, Caitlin Keiper; edited by Melanie Zimmerman; proofread by Michelle Levigne

For additional copies or customer service inquiries, please e-mail west.customer.service@thomson.com.

ISBN 978-0-314-28301-6

Mat #41308882

DEDICATION

This book is dedicated to all the parents and children who are facing difficult times; I sincerely hope you find assistance and solace in the pages of this book.

I also dedicate this book to my family who supports me in all my endeavors, loves me unconditionally, and puts up with all my foibles. I could not do this without you.

When it comes to family law cases and looking at the big picture, special recognition for the assistance he has provided me in the past belongs to my friend, and although he knows it not, *my mentor*, Gerald Reed.

Special thanks as well to Kristen Lindeman (who first gave me the opportunity to become an author), Caitlin Keiper, my project manager and advocate in obtaining approval for this venture, and those at Thomson Reuters who supported my submission for this project and assisted me through publication.

CONTENTS

Introduction

What Is the Part of the Protagonist?

If you are reading this book, you are most likely either contemplating a custody battle or are already in one. You are also likely either seeking custody or defending your custodial position. So, whether you are the father or the mother; the custodial parent or non-custodial parent; antagonist or adversary; plaintiff or defendant, the information contained in this book should be equally relevant for all.

Ideally, you are *contemplating* a custody case and as such, this book is designed to help you prepare for what is to come. However, if the battle has already been brought to you, fear not, preparation in and of itself does not victory make. A successful custody case has many elements: preparation, evidence, facts, presentation, the best interest of the child, and you—the protagonist.

Preparation

This book is designed to help you prepare both initially for a custody case as well as give you information to plan and set up the elements listed above to obtain a successful result. However, this book is not designed to advise you legally; that is the province of your attorney. Nor is this book designed to guarantee success. Success simply cannot be guaranteed. However, if you prepare, plan, obtain the necessary evidence, present the facts in the light most favorable to you and represent the best interest of your child, your chances of success are much improved.

Retaining an Attorney

Hiring a knowledgeable and skilled attorney is vital and may be one of the most important decisions you may ever make for both yourself and your child. A skilled and experienced attorney will be able to assist you in your trial preparation, direct you as hurdles arise along the way, advise you in the intricate web of decision making that may ensue during the pendency of your case, and ultimately, present your case to the court.

Doctor and lawyer shows abound on television and provide a distorted view of both the professions and the professionals. Therefore, you should expect neither a television-like trial nor a television-like attorney. However, the real life comparisons between a doctor and lawyer do exist. There are general practice physicians, neurologists, orthopedists, surgeons, and the like, in the medical field. Likewise, there are general practice lawyers, appellate lawyers, criminal lawyers, family lawyers, and lawyers who combine complementary legal disciplines to assist you. You should choose as best suits your needs.

In obtaining your attorney, you should explore your options and look for an attorney who best fits with you and your needs. You should retain an attorney with whom you are comfortable; one you can work with for what may be a protracted amount of time.

Using This Book

The information and documents provided in this book are not designed to be all-inclusive, but rather, provide a starting point and quick preparation guide to be used in conjunction with your attorney's aid and legal advice.

Whether you are a single parent, a divorcing parent, or even a grandparent seeking custody, I hope that this book brings you a better sense of the task before you and ultimately a better chance of success.

1

CHOOSING YOUR BATTLE:
Sole Custody or Joint Custody?

To try to encompass the myriad reasons you may be seeking custody of your child would be an exercise in futility. To expedite the issue, I will assume it is in your child's best interest that you have custody. But what kind of custody are you seeking?

There are two types of custody: joint and sole custody. After many years of experience and hundreds of cases, it appears that these two words are the most misunderstood of all family law concepts. Of the two, the most misrepresented is that of "joint custody."

Time and time again, my prospective and current clients sit down with me at the initial consultation with a definite understanding of what joint custody is. And time and time again, they are wrong. Typical misconceptions include:

- Joint custody means equal time with my child
- Joint custody means I have equal "say" with my child
- Joint custody means I keep my "rights"
- Joint custody means I do not have to pay child support
- Joint custody means I will not receive child support

Joint Custody

What joint custody or "parenting" really means is that the parents will "jointly parent" pursuant to a specific court order, agreement, or plan.

Many courts throughout the country have adopted standardized language and have form orders frequently used in a particular district. These may be available to you at the courthouse or from your attorney. However, the standardized language of such forms rarely fits all situations and the attorney or judge may modify each agreement on a case-by-case basis.

The essence of joint parenting is typically delineated as follows:

Joint Decisions. Both parents acknowledge that in matters of major concern, including but not limited to education, religious training, extraordinary medical care, and extracurricular activities, the parties will consult with each other and make every effort to reach vital decisions jointly. As the physical custodian, the mother shall apprise the father of the necessity of making such a vital decision, and the father shall do likewise when the need for a decision arises while the children are in his physical possession. In the event the parties do not agree as to a decision regarding areas of major concern, the parties shall submit their dispute to mediation as set forth below.

As you can see in this example, the education, religious training, extraordinary medical care, and extracurricular activities are areas of "consultation" to ultimately be decided together by the parents in this example. If no consensus can be reached, the parties are to attempt mediation with a third party as is more specifically detailed in the mediation section of the joint parenting agreement/order. Ultimately, if no agreement can be reached, the parties may return to court for a final decision. Therefore, the more mundane items such as bed times, video game selection, homework times, and television viewing rules would not necessarily be subject to joint decisions. Typically, if the child is in your care, the child lives by your rules.

On the other hand, before the child is held back a grade, enrolled in private school, baptized into a certain religion, has an operation, or allowed to race motocross, the primary caregiver or physical custodian (in the example above—the mother) must consult with and reach an agreement with the non-custodial parent (in this case—the father) before a final decision is made.

If a child or parents have additional needs, problems, or issues, the court can certainly modify any or all of these categories by expanding, defining, or even dividing the control of such categories.

The remaining portion of a joint parenting agreement or parenting order outlines the rest of the rules, rights, and responsibilities of each parent. Of these, the most important is that of the visitation or *custodial time* of each parent. As stated earlier, joint parenting does not mean "equal time," but it can. The visitation schedule defines the time both parents have with the children. The schedule itself usually specifically defines one of the parties' time and the other party receives the remaining time. For simplicity, if the mother is the primary custodial parent, the father's time is defined and carved out of the mother's time.

A typical schedule for a non-custodial parent sets forth holidays, special days, and summer visitation. Additionally, it will set forth a routine schedule such as every other weekend and one day per week as set forth below.

Weekly and Weekend Custodial Periods (Visitation): The father shall have visitation every Wednesday from 5:00 p.m. until 9:00 a.m. (or at the beginning of school) on Thursday and on alternate weekends from 5:00 p.m. on Friday until 5:00 p.m. Sunday beginning the first weekend after the entry of this order.

However, it could just as easily set forth an "equal" time schedule such as:

Weekly and Weekend Custodial Periods (Visitation): The father shall have visitation every other week beginning at 5:00 p.m. on Friday and continuing until the following Friday at 5:00 p.m. and on alternating weeks thereafter beginning the first Friday after the entry of this order.

As you can see, virtually all terms and conditions, including visitation can be modified as appropriate under the circumstances. The real issue in joint parenting agreements is that of the indication of the *principal residential custodian* or *primary custodian*.

This is the crux of the matter when it comes to joint parenting agreements and orders. Who is more suited to be the primary custodian and what does it mean to you?

To start with, it may be the difference between paying and receiving child support. As usual, there is no hard and fast rule, but typically, the person with the custodial designation receives the child support, if any. A more comprehensive discussion of child support determination is in Chapter 8 as the trial process and judge's rationale is more fully explained.

As related to the more base issue of "custody," being named primary custodian in a joint parenting agreement or order has to do with the day-to-day decision making and the raising of your child. Obviously, if you spend more time with your child, you will be more involved (or should be) with the education, morals, ethics, rules, and all other issues regarding the way your child is raised and nurtured. Likewise, and most importantly, you will be (or should be) the one to take the lead in the decision-making process. As set forth in the example above regarding joint parenting—*As the physical custodian, the mother shall apprise the father of the necessity of making such a vital decision*—it will be the primary custodian or physical custodian to bring most, if not all major issues to the attention of the non-custodial parent.

For example, a routine doctor appointment is just that, routine, and not requisite of a *joint decision*. But if after consultation, the doctor is recommending, for example, surgery, the mother, (the primary custodian in this case), must then inform the father of the diagnosis and together the parties must agree on how to proceed. In resolving the matter, they can of course take the doctor's advice, they can seek other opinions, or wait as they see fit—so long as they *mutually* agree. On the other hand, if they cannot agree, the parties must turn to mediation to resolve the issue.

You will find a complete example of a joint parenting agreement in Appendix A of this book. Special attention should be directed to:

- **6. VISITATION**
- **11. ADDITIONAL PROVISIONS**

- **12. SCHOOL INFORMATION AND ACTIVITIES**
- **13. DISPUTE RESOLUTION, CHANGE OF CIRCUMSTANCE, AND PERIODIC REVIEW**

Therefore, if you believe you can jointly parent your child with his or her other parent, careful deliberation should be given to proceeding as such. You should consult with your attorney, confirm the laws, rights, and responsibilities in your jurisdiction regarding joint custody and proceed accordingly. However, read on: There is much in the section below on sole custody that is relevant to both the primary caregiver as well as the non-custodial parent.

Sole Custody

The number one myth about sole custody is that the non-custodial parent has no rights … wrong. Each state has specific laws regarding the rights of parents. Additionally, the Uniform Child Custody Jurisdiction Enforcement Act (UCCJEA) has been adopted by virtually every state in the union. Between your individual state law and the UCCJEA, it is virtually impossible for a non-custodial parent to be shorn of his or her rights without court intervention regarding the same.

The exception is that of a father who has not claimed his rights. Typically, this is a father of a child born outside of wedlock, and there is no admission as to paternity on a form such as the voluntary acknowledgement of paternity and/or the birth certificate. If this describes you, consult your attorney so that you may take the necessary actions to protect yourself. In any event, determination of paternity is a primary concern, but peripheral to the issue of custody as being discussed in this book.

To provide a simple definition of sole custody, one only need remove the "joint" decision making from the definition of joint parenting above. The sole custodian makes all the major decisions. When it comes to education, religious training, extraordinary medical care, extracurricular activities, or any other major issue, the sole custodian has unilateral decision-making authority. However, this does not mean he or she makes *all* the decisions. The custodial parent cannot be dictatorial in all facets of the child's life. As stated earlier, the day-to-day rules and regulations in either parent's home can vary and the idea of "your house, your rules" should be maintained (within reason) and excepting of course—major decisions. Additionally, more information on post-hearing issues is in Chapter 9 regarding the final order entered in your case.

In practice, I have read many court orders that, among other things, grant sole custody to one parent. Courts have often simply stated in a divorce or custody order that "The Petitioner, John Smith (hereinafter "Father"), is granted sole custody of the minor child." "The Respondent, Jane Smith (hereinafter "Mother"), is granted the following visitation…" with no more information or direction as to what *sole custody* means. The judge knows, the lawyers know, but all too often the parties do not. This leads to the feeling of a termination of rights or helplessness for the non-custodial parent. Having an attorney who can explain and guide you post-trial will be very helpful.

As an alternative, I prefer to submit to the judge a supplemental order or agreement of sole custody that sets forth, in plain English, the rights the non-custodial parent has. Obviously, the statutes in each state are more inclusive, but this order will assist the parties in understanding how to parent after the order is entered. You will find a complete example of a sole parenting agreement in Appendix B of this book. You should note that the shared decision making is absent in this agreement. Likewise, there is no mediation requirement.

Therefore, if you do not believe it is possible to jointly parent your child, you should proceed with presenting a case for sole custody with you named as *sole* or *custodial* parent.

Tips

1. A non-custodial parent in a *joint parent agreement* may have equal custodial time or may only have limited visitation.
2. While one parent can have *sole custody*, the parties may share equal visitation time with the children or any other visitation schedule.

3. Child support is seldom affected by an award of *joint custody* without other considerations.
4. *Joint custody* is rarely <u>imposed</u> on the parties by a judge. Joint custody is more likely to be acquired by agreement.
5. *Sole custody* does not typically terminate the non-custodial parent's rights.
6. It is vital to understand what type of custody you are asking for before you ask for it.

2

MARRIED OR SINGLE:
Does It Make a Difference?

As with most things in life, there is rarely an absolute answer; thus, the answer is no and yes. Strictly and statutorily, there is typically no difference in whether you are or were married when making a custodial determination. However, it is the facts as applied to your case that make the difference. Whether you are married to the other parent of your child is, strictly speaking, a fact. Now, what does that fact mean to you?

The Married Parents

If you are a married parent, the following typically apply:

- You are the biological or adoptive parent of the child
- You live with or have lived with the child
- Custody will be part of a larger divorce proceeding
- You already have certain vested rights regarding the child
- You have comprehensive knowledge of the other party
- You have substantial knowledge of ancillary information

For purposes of this section, I am dividing the married parents into two categories: the veteran and the novice. Please note that these categories are not meant to be derogatory or critical in the least, but are meant to more appropriately illustrate certain issues.

The veteran is not necessarily someone who has been married before, has other children, or who has otherwise "been there, done that." The veteran is someone who has been married for a while, typically five or more years (to pick an arbitrary number). This person really knows:

- himself or herself
- his or her spouse
- his or her child(ren)
- and has established themselves as adult persons

Now, the above items do not necessarily mean that the veteran is any certain age, and from my experience, age is never a guarantee of veteran status. However, assuming you are of veteran status, you have certain advantages to any other type of parent discussed herein. You will find this particularly true as you move through Chapter 3 regarding parenting issues and Chapter 4 in gathering your evidence.

The novice, on the other hand, typically has been married less than five years and has the potential for added problems such as:

- a young or infant child (particularly if the only child)
- a spouse that he or she never really knew
- a spotty knowledge of ancillary information
- uncertain employment (career establishment in progress)

The above are noteworthy, but remember, your spouse faces the same drawbacks and obstacles.

So, veterans and novices, what does the fact that you are married mean to you? Obviously, the above-referenced items, but what else? To answer that, you need to understand that each court will apply the applicable state statute that defines the "best interest of the minor child." Typically, these statutes include the following concerns:

As to the child:

- The child's age and, in some jurisdictions, gender
- The child's health, both mental and physical

- The child's relationship with siblings, if any
- The child's relationship with each parent
- The child's relationship with family and friends
- The child's routine (home, school, community, etc.)
- The preference of the child, if of a certain age or sufficient maturity
- Whether the child has been abused by a parent

As to the parents:

- The health of the parents, both mental and physical
- The behavior of the parents, both good and bad
- The lifestyle and routine of the parents
- The ability to provide for the child
- The proposed residence of the child (home, school, etc.)
- The parent who has in the past acted as primary caregiver
- The ability of proposed custodial parent to foster the relationship of the child and the proposed non-custodial parent
- The wishes of the parents

For additional information and examples, I have included the statutes from three states in Appendix C. However, a quick Internet search should allow you to find your state-specific statute, or you may request a copy from your attorney.

Given the substantial list above, there is certainly much to consider. But as to the relationship between this list and your marital status, there are only a few specific areas upon which to concentrate. The first is that of the child's relationship with each parent; as a married couple the chances that both parents are more involved (or have been), especially on a day-to-day basis, with the child are increased. Additionally, direct knowledge as to which of you has acted in the past as primary caregiver, is readily ascertainable. On a practical note, if you have not been acting as primary caregiver or as involved as perhaps you could be, now is the time to start rectifying that situation. Finally, a married couple has (or had) likely established a routine with and for the child.

The Single Parents

For purposes of this section, I am dividing single parents into two categories: those who are/have lived together and those who have not lived together.

If you have lived with the other parent for a significant period of time or otherwise held yourselves out as a married couple in name or action, certain states may recognize this as a common law marriage. For the purposes of this book on *custody,* such parents are hereby unilaterally designated (by me) as married and should (if you have not already) read the first part of Chapter 2 regarding married parents.

If you have not lived with the other parent or have done so for a brief period of time only (and no longer do so), you are the true single parent.

If you are the parent with whom the child resides, you are in the best possible position to obtain and/or maintain custody. You should, almost by default, have the following in your favor: an established track record of providing for your child; an established home, school, daycare, etc., for your child; a routine your child is used to; and potentially a number of the other "best interest" factors as listed previously.

On the other hand, if you are the single parent who does not live with the child, you face a most difficult and trying case ahead. Difficult and trying—yes; is it impossible—no. Having set forth the court's primary concerns as to the "best interest" of the minor child, you know what you are up against. However, if you are seeking custody at this time, it is likely you have reason. As such, you will have to capitalize on those issues and build your case accordingly.

The Preborn Child

There is one more kind of parent, a kind that could fall into any of the four categories set forth above, and that is the parent of an unborn/preborn child. Assuming natural conception, the female parent is most assuredly the biological mother of the child. However, until the child is born, the biological father is unknown/unproven (seldom is a DNA-parentage test taken during the pregnancy). However, mother and father alike often are concerned about the custody and visitation arrangements of the unborn child.

If you find yourself in this situation, keep in mind that the statutes on custody do not allow judicially awarded custody pre-birth (barring exigent circumstances). However, if you are married, both parents have statutorily defined rights. Alternatively, if you are not married, typically only the mother has such defined rights. You should consult an attorney immediately as to your individual rights and how you should proceed during the gestational period. After the birth, all considerations as to the best interest of the minor child should then apply.

Tips

1. The more that information you are privy to, the better position you are in to build your case.
2. If your child has not yet been born, comprehensive advice regarding your rights should be sought as soon as possible.

3

ASSESSING YOUR CASE:
What Kind of Parent Am I?

You should now have a better understanding of the relationship you are in with the other parent and the relationship to custody. Likewise, you should better understand what custody is and what kind of custody you desire. But what kind of parent are you? What kind of parent is the other party? By dissecting these two issues, you can better prepare both your offense and defense. Further, you can identify your shortfalls and work to reduce or eliminate them.

Prior Primary Caregiver

One of the strongest arguments made in the courts regarding custody is that of who has acted as primary caregiver of the child. The person who can make this argument is typically in the best position to maintain the designation of primary caregiver.

However, if this has not been you in the past, the typical corollary argument you can use is this: The person who has been acting as primary caregiver is not doing the job well or appropriately.

Below you will find a checklist included as part of Appendix D titled Comprehensive Custody Questionnaire. Think about each category and enter the percentage of involvement each of you have had regarding the indicated tasks and activities.

Infant/Toddler Care

Activity/Responsibility	% Mother	% Father
Feeding	_____	_____
Diaper changes	_____	_____
Holding/comforting	_____	_____
Bathing	_____	_____
Brushing teeth	_____	_____
Dressing	_____	_____
Put to bed	_____	_____
Reading stories	_____	_____
Discipline	_____	_____
Explain: _____		
Other: Examples: _____		

Health Care

Activity/Responsibility	% Mother	% Father
Doctor visits	_____	_____
Dental visits	_____	_____
Orthodontist visits	_____	_____
Taking care of child when sick	_____	_____
Other: Examples: _____		

Daily Care

Activity/Responsibility	% Mother	% Father
Preparing meals	_____	_____
Grocery shopping	_____	_____
Laundry	_____	_____
Clothes shopping	_____	_____
Shopping for school supplies	_____	_____
Arranging childcare/daycare	_____	_____
Taking to/picking up from daycare	_____	_____
Teaching values	_____	_____
Teaching manners	_____	_____

Assignment of child's chores
(or enforcement)   _____   _____
Playing indoors   _____   _____
        Examples: _____
Playing outdoors   _____   _____
        Examples: _____
Cleaning home   _____   _____
Other: Examples: _____

School Years

Activity/Responsibility	% Mother	% Father
Bathing	_____	_____
Styling hair	_____	_____
Haircuts	_____	_____
Preparing lunches	_____	_____
Dressing	_____	_____
Brushing teeth (help or reminding)	_____	_____
Bedtime enforcement	_____	_____
Reading stories, books	_____	_____
Helping with homework	_____	_____
Taking to/picking up from school	_____	_____
Taking to/picking up from extracurricular activities	_____	_____
Teacher's conferences	_____	_____
Attending open houses	_____	_____
School volunteering	_____	_____
Attending PTA/PTO meetings	_____	_____

        Examples: _____

Discipline   _____   _____
        Explain: _____
Other: Examples: _____

Extracurricular Activities

Activity/Responsibility	% Mother	% Father
Taking to/picking up from church/activities	_____	_____
Taking to/picking up from sports activities	_____	_____

Coaching   _____   _____
Taking to/picking up from lessons   _____   _____
Hosting birthday parties   _____   _____
Other: Examples: _____

Given the above, how do you rate? If you are firmly in the lead, you should work to maintain your advantage. If you are behind, this is typically *not* the time to try to commandeer the raising of your child. Instead, you should carefully consider the following factors.

First, determine if it is feasible to improve or assume a particular task. For example, if you work the second shift at work, you likely work a 3:00 p.m. to 11:00 p.m. schedule. Therefore, it is virtually impossible to feed the child dinner, help with homework, or tuck him or her into bed with a story. However, you can, and should do this activity on your days off.

Second, determine how relevant any given activity is to your case. Trying to "un-ring the bell," as it were, is a waste of time and likely a red flag to the other party. Instead, insert yourself into those areas to minimize the advantage your spouse may have on a given area. For example, if you start trying to select and purchase all the clothing for a child, you may run afoul of the child's style and his or her routine. Instead, pick up a new pair of shoes or boots—something they need or desire. Alternatively, buy the accessories for an activity and then do that activity with your child (for example, buy the appropriate outerwear and safety equipment and take your child on bike rides, or whatever "adult" hobby/activity your child emulates that can bring you closer together).

Third, build on everything else. Start attending the parent/teacher conferences, go on a field trip, take a day off work (when the child is not in school—such as a school holiday) and spend it with your child instead of relying on a babysitter. Start making an effort to play ball in the yard or have a tea party instead of just watching television with him or her. In this way, win or lose, you are establishing a better relationship with your child that will pay dividends in the years to come.

Obviously, if you already do all of the above, keep it up and document it. You cannot rely on the other party to admit the truth to your involvement. Further, as time passes, you memory will fade as to specifics. In any event, each party should begin a divorce journal as is discussed more fully in Chapter 4.

Ability to Provide

In looking at the ability to provide and care for the children, the following issues apply:

- The health of the parents, both mental and physical
- The financial ability to provide for the child
- The lifestyle and routine of the parents

Perhaps the most-argued issue between parents is that of the mental health and stability of the parents. Since the late 1980s, depression has been a major factor, and since early in the 2000s, the diagnosis of bipolar disorder has found prominence. Technically, both are controllable by medication. Assuming proper medical care and evidence that such medicines are effective, courts are reluctant to assign significant weight to such medical diagnosis for you or the other parent. Likewise, other mental conditions, in and of themselves, do not make or break a case. What matters is how these afflictions affect the parent's ability to parent or how they affect (or have affected) the children. Additionally, does this parent acknowledge the problem, and maintain and comply with the medical treatment and medications? All too often, depressed or bi-polar individuals stop treatment when they feel "cured," which is a natural by-product of the medicine. A rollercoaster of treatment and behavior then ensues. If you are under treatment, continue it per your doctor's instructions and show the judge you are stable. If it is the other parent, document the ups and downs, and use the instability to your advantage.

Unlike mental health issues, physical infirmities are rarely controlled by medications. A prosthesis is an aid, not a cure. A blind or deaf person can function fully and successfully in life and certainly can raise a child. The court cannot and will not discriminate against you based on any such affliction. However, does this physical issue create difficulties for the child? Is it in the best interest of the child to be raised by this individual versus the other? This is the pivotal concern regarding a court's consideration of physical limitations of a parent.

Perhaps the most groundless (and absurd) concern raised by any prospective party is that "I can afford to raise the child but he or she cannot." Financially speaking, this matter is made moot by child support. If you do not have custody, you will likely be paying child support, and *presto*, the other parent can afford to raise the child. Despite this, financial issues are still a concern, but usually in a less direct manner. Where and how you spend your money is more important than how much of it you have. Do you spend your money foolishly? Are food, shelter, and other necessities the primary use of your money? Do you have a gambling or drug problem eating away at your income? Do you put your child and his or her needs first financially? Does the other parent? These are the main points a judge will look to in ascertaining financial responsibility.

The use of your money leads naturally to the next issue: the lifestyle and routine of the parent(s). Assuming you live with (or have lived with) the other parent, a certain routine was enjoyed by your children. This routine includes the previously discussed and listed primary custodial activities and tasks with which each party and children were involved. One of the key issues here is that of each parent's employment or career. Almost everyone's life is predominated by his or her work schedule. This schedule typically dictates your routine. One of the hardest custody cases involves the parent who works the third shift, particularly if this work schedule is a permanent arrangement. Remember, a custody case is about your child, not necessarily you. The child's schedule will likely include school as his or her primary focus each day, homework, food, and normal sleep arrangements. So adjusting your schedule to most benefit your child will likewise benefit your claim for custody.

The category of *lifestyle* is more esoteric. Almost any characteristic, personal idiosyncrasies, hobbies, or other facet of your life could be used against you or to your advantage. Attorneys are spin doctors (but you knew that already), and they can and will make what they can of any given fact. Does the mother drink alcohol? Maybe she is a closet alcoholic. Does she drink in front of the kids? Maybe she is conditioning the children to believe this is acceptable behavior. Does the father swear and use profanity in front of the kids? Maybe he is corrupting their morals. Does he swear and use profanity *at* the kids? Maybe he is verbally abusive. Does the mother go out every weekend with the girls? Maybe she is irresponsible or puts her enjoyment before the care of the children? Does the father play in every sports league he can join? Maybe his priorities are misdirected. Only by looking at your opponent in all aspects, can you search out the points of attack and capitalize on them. Likewise, if you are not putting your child's needs first, do so now before your actions are used against you.

Behavior of the Parent

The court will look at both good and bad behavior of the parent. Good behavior is a relatively straightforward concept and will likely encompass the involvement in the tasks and activities discussed previously. In a nutshell, you should present at trial all your positive qualities as related to custody.

On the other hand, nobody is perfect and each of us has his or her own bad qualities and bad behaviors. If you feel otherwise, please refer to the section above regarding mental health. In any event, you must reduce, restrict, and revisit any of your bad behaviors to moderate the effect these may have on your case in chief. Consulting your attorney will be invaluable in this area.

We can now turn to the other party's bad behavior. Bad behavior, as previously discussed, could be that of alcohol consumption, verbal abuse, or myriad other evils. As such, a comprehensive dissertation on such is impossible in this venue. However, typical bad behaviors include, but are not limited to abuse (of a party or child), abandonment, moral turpitude, criminal acts, substance abuse, alienation, and neglect.

Abuse

Abuse comes in many forms and is usually directed toward the other parent, toward the child, or both. The abuse may be emotional, physical, or sexual. Each form of abuse has specific nuances that should be considered as you prepare your case.

Abuse toward the other parent, be it physical, emotional, or sexual, may be viewed any number of ways. First, abuse toward the other parent may be indicative of future abuse toward the child. By dissecting the nature of the abuse, each facet of such abuse can be correlated to future parenting. For example, men are often accused of being sexist or negative toward women. Likewise, women are often accused of belittling or emasculating men. Such behavior may be argued as evidence of future similar abuse or mistreatment as the child reaches adolescence (and become young men and women) and who may become the subject of this verbal treatment by a custodial parent.

Physical abuse is substantially similar, although arguably more damaging. If a child witnesses abuse of his parent by the other, there is the arguably emotional damage. This can be of particular import when a child is raised in this environment and is taught that this is appropriate behavior. Additionally, it can be argued that the abuse of an adult parent will eventually lead to abuse of the minor.

Current abuse of the child is of greater concern as it affects custody. The abuse a parent has or is suffering should end upon separation. Additionally, the adult should have the ability to take self-preservative actions. A child does not. Therefore, if your child is suffering or has suffered abuse, particularly physically or sexually, seek immediate relief and assistance. Again, having an attorney to assist will prove invaluable.

Abandonment

All too often, one party is forced, either by court order or self-preservation, to vacate the family residence. However, this is not necessarily *abandonment*. Abandonment is that of absence coupled with disinterest, among other things. If you intend to allege abandonment, documentation is essential. This will be discussed more thoroughly in Chapter 4. However, for the purposes of this section, it is of greater value to discuss the defense against such a claim as opposed to the prosecution of the issue.

As already discussed, maintaining the status quo for the child is of great import to a custody case. Therefore, more often than not, you should seek to stay in the familiar residence during the pendency of your case. However, if factors combine to force you from the residence, it is typically advisable that you keep the child with you. By moving the child with you, you immediately begin to establish a routine and comfort level in the new location. Unfortunately, this is where the custody battle becomes most ugly. Rarely does the other party take such action without objection.

However, we are discussing abandonment. Therefore, if the situation requires separation from the child, you should take every opportunity to stay involved with the child and maintain as many routines as possible. If you are completely denied access to your child, you should seek legal remedy and document your efforts at maintaining a relationship with your child. By doing so, any claim that you abandoned your child should be moot.

Finally, you can use such interference with your relationship to your advantage. Such behavior is often viewed as alienation of affection or evidence that the other party cannot or will not foster a relationship between you and the child, which are important factors in determining the "best interest" of the minor child.

Alienation of Affection

Many jurisdictions recognize a legally defined cause of action called "alienation of affection." Here, I am not using it as such. I am incorporating this issue along with that of the custodial parent's ability to foster the relationship with the non-custodial parent.

I am defining *alienation of affection* as a bad behavior by a parent wherein he or she attempts to poison the mind of the child against the other parent. This is routinely done by one parent's systematic attack on the other parent by continually speaking negatively about that parent to the child; punishing the child for talking about or otherwise being engaged with the other parent; or intentionally interfering or denying contact between the child and other parent. Parents have also used positive reinforcement on occasion to accomplish similar results by promising the child rewards or more attractive activities if the child chooses one parent over the other. No parent should practice any of the above activities because it may be used against you and, more importantly, it can be detrimental to the child.

Conversely, the court will look to that parent who will foster the relationship with the other parent as part of the determination as to who will be awarded custody. Therefore, any action you take should be consistent with the best interest of the child.

Moral Turpitude

The issue of an adulterous affair and/or post-separation romantic relationship often finds its way into the facts of a courtroom drama. These issues may be important to a divorce proceeding but are not always related to custody. To be relevant, they must affect the child in a relatively direct manner. For example, a discrete affair that causes the dissolution of a marriage may have no impact on the children except insofar as his or her parents are no longer married. In the alternative, if the child is witnessing a different man or woman exiting the parent's bedroom weekend after weekend, there is more likely than not a very real and negative effect on the child (let alone the physical danger to the child in having strangers in the home).

Other moral issues are perhaps more subjective. Sexism, racism, religion/atheism, or any other ethical or moral considerations where you and the other parent disagree can be areas of contention. Determining if such beliefs or behaviors are detrimental to the child will have to be presented to the judge for final consideration.

Criminal Acts

Closely related to moral and ethical issues is that of criminal acts. Any criminal act, violent, or non-violent crimes, if done in the presence of the minor child, may affect the moral and ethical character of the child. Furthermore, and perhaps more importantly, it could directly endanger the child.

However, criminal behavior, unlike other behavior, need not be conducted in the presence of the child to have a very real effect on the child. For example, illegal drug use may directly affect the parent's ability to care for a child, but even possession of said drugs in your home is still a danger. The child could ingest the drugs, another criminal could break in and steal the drugs, and of course, the parent could be arrested for possession of the drugs. None of the above bodes well for a custodial parent.

Further, a criminal history may show a propensity for crime, immaturity, and lack of good judgment. Any of these factors could be detrimental to the best interest of the minor child.

Substance Abuse

Substance abuse includes not only the abuse of alcohol and illegal drugs, but also the abuse of valid prescriptions drugs. Alcohol is the usual substance that is alleged to be abused. All too often, one party drinks more than the other approves, but is it abuse of alcohol? Documentation and evidence are the key in successfully proving abuse of alcohol. Such evidence usually includes items such as a record of past treatment, DUI records, and/or qualified lay and professional opinions. Such evidence is also usually required for allegations of abuse of prescription and illegal drugs.

Neglect

Neglect, by definition, is omitting, failing, or forbearing to do a thing that can or should be done. It may also mean absence of care or attention (pursuant to *Black's Law Dictionary*). However, in raising a child, a parent may be neglectful without behaving in a manner sufficient to meet said definition. Neglect in a custody case should be more loosely interpreted to mean more neglectful than you. In other words, you should attempt to prove you are the better, more attentive parent. Having completed the activity/responsibility part of the Comprehensive Custody Questionnaire earlier in this chapter, you should already have a strong understanding of your strengths and weaknesses.

However, there are truly neglectful parents out there. These parents have failed to provide proper nutrition and health care for the child, the education of the child may be suffering, or the parent may have failed to properly supervise the child, resulting in injury. Further, any other number of other possibilities may exist when raising a child. In a true neglect case, evidence should be readily available and exploited to your advantage.

Tips

1. Be realistic in assessing your chances of success.
2. Even if you are not successful in obtaining custody, becoming a better parent to your child will benefit both you and your child.
3. Custody is about your child and what is in his or her best interest—not what is in your best interest.
4. If custody was determined based on finances, no one would be awarded custody—children are expensive.
5. If you need help for mental issues, seek appropriate help. Being healthy will serve your child better than a custodial award to a parent in need of treatment.
6. You are under a virtual microscope and everything you do may be called into question.
7. Playing "dirty tricks" on the other parent is unlikely to assist your case in the long term.

4

GATHERING EVIDENCE:
Can I Prove It?

Even if you have all the facts in your favor, they will be useless to you unless you can present them to the judge for consideration. The only way these facts will be provided to the judge (excepting stipulations) is through testimony. From that testimony, facts will be elicited via direct examination, cross examination, and the entry of exhibits. Therefore, you must gather your facts, document said facts so that you may testify, and obtain documentary and illustrative exhibits to present at trial.

You are your own best witness. It is your case to make; it is your memory that will be tested; it is your veracity that will be measured; and it is the evidence you bring to support your claim that the judge will use to make his final ruling.

Divorce Journal

To make you a better witness, I recommend you begin keeping a divorce journal. This is the simplest of ways to assist you in bringing your case effectively to court as well as helping you during the actual trial. You can use a simple notebook, your smartphone, or any other item that you can carry with you to keep notes. It need only be something that can be printed out/transferred and provided to your attorney. A brief sample of such a journal is in Appendix E.

The journal need not be particularly neat, only comprehensive. Every day from this day forward should contain an entry with the day's date. Enter any information relevant to your child and your custody case as it happens for that day. Do not include how you "feel" or your "hopes and dreams"; this journal is related strictly to custody and may be required to be turned over to the other party in the discovery process. So bear in mind that what you write may be used against you.

As you begin your journal, you will likely see trends begin to take shape. As this happens, your memory as to previous incidents, activities, or other items of import may come to mind. Therefore, you may also wish to prepare a pre-journal history or timeline. Much like the divorce journal, this document will contain a chronological account of important information. Such a timeline may be very detailed or relatively sparse depending on the incidents in question or the quality of your memories. Such a timeline may look something like the following:

- February 14, 2001: Married in Las Vegas
- April 1, 2001: Baby John born
- Summer 2001: Husband deployed to Korea for three months
- Easter 2002: Wife left child with husband for two months to live with her parents during depression episode
- Summer 2002: Bought new house
- May 5, 2003: Baby Susan born
- May 21, 2003: Wife graduated with master's degree
- Spring 2005: Major argument over public school versus private school for children
- August 1, 2006: Husband arrested for DUI
- October 15, 2006: Husband's second arrest for DUI
- Fall 2006: Wife treated inpatient for depression
- Spring 2007: Husband treated inpatient for alcohol abuse
- 2008 (Mid-Spring to Mid-Summer): Parties separated
- Summer 2008: Parties reconciled
- January 2009: Parties filed for bankruptcy
- Etc.

Ultimately, by using such documents as the timeline and journal, you will be able to establish patterns, point to specific instances in your case, as well as refresh your memory as needed.

Pictures

We have heard it a million times—a picture is worth a thousand words. Nowhere could this be more true than in court! Permit me a couple words and I will demonstrate.

Assume a picture of your child's birthday party, you could likely testify to the following:

- how old your child is in the picture
- who was there (and who should have been)
- who planned it
- where it took place
- what happened during the party
- who was intoxicated
- what happened after

If you answered fully just those categories, you would likely surpass the 1,000-word count and would have presented to the court a substantial, and perhaps very pertinent, amount of information.

Pictures, therefore, can be of great assistance. Additionally, you should consider pictures that demonstrate or prove multiple facets of your case to expedite and reinforce your case.

Event Pictures: These are pictures of events in your life or your child's life that are relevant to custody. The birthday party mentioned above may be relevant to show you are the primary organizer/caregiver, that the other parent was absent or intoxicated, or the relationship the child has with friends and family. Likewise, other events such as vacations and graduations can be similarly helpful. On the other hand, do not forget to consider an accident as an event as well. If the other parent thought it a good idea to have your child jump off a merry-go-round and that jump resulted in a broken arm, show the picture.

Demonstrative Pictures: These pictures demonstrate the status of your life. Many times these pictures are taken for the sole purpose of the custody trial. A picture of your home shows the court where you live and helps the court understand the lifestyle and routine of the child. A picture of a child's bedroom demonstrates the type of decorator (nurturer, housekeeper, etc.) you are and helps the court better understand the child. A picture of your street helps the court understand your neighborhood. These pictures also help the court compare and contrast your house and neighborhood to those of the other parent. As a practice note, nothing says you cannot drive by and take pictures of the other party's house, or even inside—if invited!

Evidentiary Pictures: These pictures are typically used to attempt to prove one or more of your allegations. Examples of such pictures would be a photograph of the other parent snorting cocaine, passed out drunk, or a mug shot from an arrest report. On the other hand, they can also be affirmative in nature. Such photos may be of you helping your child study or learn to ride a bicycle. However, such pictures should not be staged.

Videotape: In my experience, most attorneys are not partial to videotape, however, in certain cases it is vital. Pictures are preferred for court use and are easier to handle. However, if videotape is necessary or is already in existence, make sure that the video is necessary and a picture of the incident will not suffice. Further, there can be legal issues if you are recording without knowledge of all parties. Consult your attorney before taping any new incidents.

Documents

Everybody has seen a movie or television show where the protagonist is covertly rifling through a desk or slipping a flash drive into the USB port of a computer. In a custody case, this is not that far-fetched. The only caveat to this scenario is that it is imperative that you do not violate the law. Having legitimate access to the home, desk, or computer is one thing; going rogue is another. If you have any questions regarding your upcoming recognizance mission, consult your attorney.

Assuming therefore legitimate, non-felonious access to documents, you should consider gathering the following to both bolster your case as well as contradict the other parties:

Phone Records: If you do not already have your phone company detailing both incoming and outgoing phone calls, do so. If your provider cannot or will not provide such a bill, other carriers such as Vonage may be the solution. Switching to such a plan and keeping your existing number (when possible) is a covert way to gain this valuable information.

In any event, being able to prove how many times the opposing party called can be invaluable. Many times a parent will claim you have denied phone contact between them and the child. If your records show all incoming calls and the duration, such allegations are easily refuted. Likewise, if you are being harassed by a multitude of phone calls per day, these too will be evident. Finally, you may wish to subpoena the other party's phone records to obtain this information or to show to whom the other party is talking, for how long, and when.

Internet and Computer Records: First, copying the contents of a computer's hard drive is a relatively simple exercise. However, make sure you include Internet search history and any "private" files, if you can find them. However, laws vary from state to state and proper consultation with legal counsel is a must before proceeding in this area.

On the other hand, copying a computer's hard drive is not the only way to obtain pertinent computer and Internet information. Monitoring the other party's Facebook, Myspace, Twitter, or other social network is also highly advisable. Print any new or relevant entries as they appear so you have a hard copy. This is also a great place to obtain photographs. Warning—your accounts and entries on your social networks can just as easily be used against you. Finally, even if you do not have access to the other party's accounts, it may be possible to subpoena the records directly from the Internet provider.

Internet Searches: The Internet is a part of virtually everyone's life, and with minimal search time you should be able to gather any available personal information on the other person—just "Google" them. Additionally, many websites may also be informational. Search the Sex Offender Registry for your area. Are there sexual predictors in your neighborhood? The other party's neighborhood? Search the "dead beat dad" registry. Search dating websites for the other parent. Search blogs and other related sites that the other parent might belong to for additional information.

Correspondence: Correspondence can include computer and Internet communications such as e-mail, text, and social networks as discussed above. However, old-fashioned snail mail, love notes, or even a suicide note should not be overlooked and should be included in your documentation. Even the nasty message written on your bathroom mirror in lipstick can and should be preserved (by photograph) for future use.

Affirmative items can include the Mother's Day and Father's Day cards with the added note of what a "Truly great parent you are..." as signed by the other parent. Thank you notes from a school teacher or Boy/Girl Scout troop leader may also be helpful.

In any event, all communications between you and the other parent should be saved or preserved.

Public and Semi-Public Records: There are potentially a number of sources for records that may be relevant to your case. The following are a few possibilities:

<u>Criminal Records</u>: A criminal record is usually public record, if you know where to look. Many counties now have public accessible websites for their jurisdiction. Simply logging on and entering a name can provide a plethora of information. Additionally, your attorney may have access to nationwide database (or he may routinely work with a private investigator that can obtain this information). If your search proves fruitful, a request to the police department will usually lead to a copy of the entire report.

<u>Freedom of Information Act</u>: Police records are also available under the Freedom of Information Act. Additionally, a request for 911 calls

to a specific address or neighborhood can also be made. When comparing the safety of a neighborhood, it may be rather enlightening to find out how many drug arrests, thefts, assaults, or even murders have happened within few block radius of the subject residence. You may even be surprised at how many times the police have been to the other parent's residence.

<u>Court Records</u>: Running the name of the other parent at various courthouses may also yield additional information besides a criminal record. Perhaps the other parent has been sued, previously divorced, had a child taken away by the authorities, or is in foreclosure and about to lose his or her home. Any or all of the above may be very valuable information to your case. Additionally, a search of federal records can yield information on fraud cases, federal drug charges/convictions, or even bankruptcy records.

<u>School Records</u>: You should obtain a copy of your child's school records, daycare records, camp records, or any other related documentation regarding your child. A report card can show not only how the child is performing but also a number of other important facts. It will likely discuss his attitude and participation. It will show how often he or she was tardy or absent. Daycare records, on the other hand, will show times and dates of attendance and likely who picked up and dropped off the child. It may also show how often a child was picked up excessively late.

Many schools today also have a homework planner. The child's homework will be written in each day and many teachers request that a parent sign off each night upon completion. Additionally, the teacher may write notes to the parent regarding positive and negative issues. This planner should be copied periodically to help you prove any combination of relevant information in your case such as:

- who is helping with homework (if anyone)
- is the homework being completed
- what are the problems the child is having

Finally, many schools participate in state ranking programs. Commonly referred to as a "school's report card," these printouts are available on the Internet and can be used to compare different schools or school districts.

Bills and Home Documents: This category of documents will likely be obtained in one of two ways; either you are in the home and the documents are readily available to you or, they will need to be subpoenaed by your attorney from either the other side or the source directly.

If you share the home, you should have access to documents such as prior tax returns, mortgage documents, loan documents, bills, and debts. Any or all could contain relevant information. It should be relatively easy to take a day when the other party is not home and make copies of all such documents. The originals should be returned, since both of you have (presumably) equal right to the documents. Your copies should then be stored safely out of the home.

Created Documents: An attorney or party, particularly when preparing for trial, may find it necessary to create demonstrative evidence or documents. However, this does not mean they are fabricated from whole cloth. The pictures discussed above, taken to show where you live, are one type of created document. Another would be a color-coded calendar where you demonstrate which days you had possession of your child in an effort to show your routine involvement (or lack thereof) with your child. These documents are of great use to combine and simplify data to be presented to the judge.

Phone Taps: Phone taps are great in the movies but violate both federal and state laws. Do not do it. If you believe this type of surveillance is necessary, contact your local authorities and allow them to investigate within the bounds of the law.

Witnesses

Having at least one witness to bolster your case is almost always advisable. Not only does the witness support what you have testified to, he or she may add vital evidence outside your direct knowledge. This often avoids hearsay problems. Finally, expert witnesses can also be beneficial when their specialized knowledge is required.

Family: The most popular and typical witness is a family member. Grandparents, aunts, uncles, brothers, and sisters usually are the most likely to have been around you and your child. They are also more likely to put themselves out there for you. Granted, they also have the most vested interests. Thus, care should be taken to make sure that they cannot be painted as unduly prejudiced in the matter. The relationship that family has to your child is also a significant factor the court uses in making a determination as to "best interest" of the child.

Friends: Friends can be a great help or a great hindrance. If your friend is your drinking buddy or some type of undesirable, you may wish to rethink calling him or her as a witness on your behalf. However, if the value of his or her testimony outweighs the possible negative impact on your case, proceed. Assuming no such negative concerns, the friends often have more current and relevant information than even family members. Friends often supply opinions of both parties, have witnessed you in your capacity as parent, and can vouch for your character. Since their relationship to you is less intimate than family, a court may also assign more weight to their "honest" opinion of you.

Opposing Witnesses: Do not overlook the other parent's witnesses. Much information may be available by deposing these witnesses and cross-examining them at trial. You should provide as much information as you have about any such witness to your attorney so he can prepare accordingly. Further, you should not overestimate loyalty. Many a time, a grandparent has, in all honesty, said that the court should not give custody to their own progeny.

Neighbors: When assessing your case, do not overlook the nosy neighbor (or the very nice neighbor), yours and the other parent's. You would be surprised at just how much they may know. They can testify to watching you play ball with your kids, teaching them to ride their bikes, or how your children play around the neighborhood. They can also testify how the other parent (or you) screams at the kids, hit the mailbox as you pulled into your driveway in a drunken stupor, or how many times the police have paid you or the other parent a visit.

Teachers: Unless your child is extremely young, chances are he or she is involved with a teacher or daycare provider. Make friends with this person. A daycare provider can testify to numerous issues regarding both the parent as well as the child. Pick-ups, drop offs, hygiene, demeanor, and overall care are often observed and noted by this person.

The child's school teacher should also remember your involvement with school activities, parent/teacher involvement, and other important issues regarding your child's education.

Additionally, daycare providers and teachers are usually mandated child abuse reporters.

Counselors: If your child is having problems, generally or because of the ongoing tug-of-war between the parents, you should seek proper care for him or her. First, this shows you are taking the lead in the medical care of you child. Second, if there is a problem, the court should be made aware of such issues and consider how a custody placement may affect the child or the treatment. Finally, the child will have (hopefully) confided in this person. The counselor may then either testify as to what the child has reported, or act as an expert witness and give an expert opinion to the court.

The Ex: It is commonly understood that my enemy's enemy is my friend. As such, you may consider contacting the other parent's previous paramours. Sometimes there is a veritable wealth of information available through such a person.

Private Investigator: Rarely is a private investigator necessary in a custody case. Unless the other parent is a complete mystery to you or is otherwise lying in such a way that other proof cannot shed the appropriate light on the necessary facts, a private investigator is usually not a good use of your money. However, if after careful consideration, you or your attorney believes it is necessary, hire a private investigator with the proper credentials and who is familiar with the court process.

Other

The examples regarding documentation and witnesses discussed above are by no means a comprehensive list of everything you may need to prove your case. However, it is a very thorough start, and it may very well be all you need. After years of practice and countless cases, one fact is universal—every custody case is unique. As such, you should gather any other necessary evidence to support your case and introduce all relevant material to the judge in a manner to best present your case.

Tips

1. Documentation is vital to your case.
2. A wealth of information can be found in family pictures.
3. The more thorough you are in obtaining documentation, the easier it will be to prove your case.
4. Ask your potential witnesses to testify early in the proceeding so that they too can gather information and refresh their memories in anticipation of trial.
5. Do not leave the leg work to your attorney—you are your best advocate.

5

DISCOVERY:
What Do They Have?

Discovery is a legal term of art that is defined within trial practice as: The pre-trial devices that can be used by one party to obtain facts and information about the case from the other party to assist the party's preparation for trial (pursuant to *Black's Law Dictionary*). In other words, it is the mechanism in which you obtain "discoverable" information from the other side, while they attempt to obtain "discoverable" information from you. Complete candor is required and an affidavit of truthfulness and full disclosure is usually required as part of said disclosures. Unlike television cases, a key fact or piece of evidence cannot be hidden and brought out for a "death blow" in the courtroom. Failure to disclose may result in that particular item or bit of information being barred from admission to the court and ultimately not considered by the judge.

Discovery usually comes in two forms, written and testimonial. Written discovery is a request (in writing) sent to the opposing party, typically in the form of such documents as a request to produce, interrogatories, and requests to admit. A written response is then returned within a specified period of time. There are, of course, slight variations from state to state and more specific requests can be made in any given cause of action. However, these are the most likely to be used in a custody case. On the other hand, testimonial discovery is usually an in-person interview or deposition.

Written Discovery

Request to Produce: This document is propounded to a party to obtain any and all relevant documentary evidence he or she anticipates using in trial. Basically, you will now turn over all the documents you gathered as referenced in Chapter 4. Likewise, you will be asking that the other parent turn over any such documents they have gathered in their defense (or for their offense). By this mechanism, you may also be able to obtain evidence you believe may exist but are unable to obtain on your own. For example, you may wish to have a copy of the other party's work schedule. Typically, only the employer and employee are privy to this document, but now, it will have to be turned over to you by the other parent. You may use it to show how that parent's work schedule (or frequent overnight travel for work) makes day-to-day care of the child virtually impossible. Therefore, if there is particular information you are seeking, make sure you ask for it in the request to produce.

Interrogatories: This is merely the legal word for questions. This document will have a number of questions for you to answer. Likewise, you will send such questions to the opposing party for him or her to answer. Many times the answers to these questions will give significant insight to the other parties' underlying case. For example, a typical question might be: *"Why do you believe the mother/father is an unfit parent? State your answer with specificity."* Upon receiving the answer, you know exactly what allegations the other parent will be making against you. You can then prepare your defense against such claims.

Request to Admit: This document is similar to the interrogatories, but instead of asking a question, it asks you to either admit or deny a statement of fact. Be warned, this is a very time-sensitive document. Failure to respond in a timely manner will result in the statements being deemed admitted. This document can be particularly useful with someone who is being evasive. Further, it may put a highly volatile issue front and center for what may be a quick resolution. For example, in an attempt to minimize the need to have the child testify, one could ask the other party to either admit or deny the following statement: "The minor child has told me, on more than one occasion, that she wished to reside with the mother." The father must either admit or deny same, and sign an affidavit to that effect. Assuming no perjury, the issue of the child's preference could be made moot.

Testimonial Discovery

Depositions: In some, but not all cases, depositions may be taken of the parties or witnesses. Depositions can be useful for many reasons, but can also be relatively expensive. Whether to take a deposition should be considered carefully with your attorney.

In most cases, only the parties are deposed. Notice is sent to each party and a stenographer or court reporter is present to record all testimony. The testimony is taken under oath and then transcribed and provided in written format to each party and their attorneys. So what should you expect? If you are being deposed, you will be sworn in by the court reporter and then asked a number of questions by the opposing party's attorney. Your attorney will be present and may object as necessary or otherwise advise you throughout the course of the deposition.

Despite your attorney being present, depositions are rarely stress-free events. You will likely feel somewhat violated before the deposition is complete as the other attorney "goes fishing" for usable information. A discovery deposition is conducted for just that reason and any area that may yield relevant information may usually be explored.

Although more unusual, witness depositions may also be taken. Like a party deposition, an attorney may use the forum to explore exactly what a witness knows and what he or she will testify to during trial. An added advantage to any deposition is that the information has now been recorded under oath. Any changes at trial to your witnesses' testimony (or your testimony as obtained in your deposition) may call into your question the truthfulness of the previous or current information/evidence as well as the overall veracity of the person testifying.

Illustrative Questions

As stated earlier, most discovery depositions are fishing expeditions. As such, you can expect questions from any quarter. However, certain areas are usually covered in some form or fashion. Likewise, certain types of questions are commonly asked to lay a foundation for proving you are or are not the parent best suited for custody. Below you will find examples of a few such questions and the subject matter the attorneys are attempting to probe.

"If you are awarded custody, what visitation schedule do you believe would be appropriate for the other parent?" is a typical question. If you respond with a very nominal amount, an argument can be made that you are unwilling to foster the relationship between the child and the parent by minimizing their relationship. If you indicate a great amount, an argument could be made that you do not believe you should really be the primary caregiver and are shirking your responsibility as a caregiver, or you do not really even want custody. Any number of such questions could then follow. Eventually, however, the attorney will likely ask, "If the other parent is awarded custody, what visitation do you believe would be appropriate for you?" If you now indicate that you should receive more visitation than the other parent, this can again bolster the argument that you are attempting to minimalize the other parent's relationship with the child. Further, if such a visitation is what was best for the child, why should the other parent not also have such a visitation schedule?

Attorneys also commonly ask, *"What is your child's teacher's name?"* This question is less difficult, but perhaps more poignant. If you do not know, just how involved in the child's schooling are you? Similarly, you can expect a question such as, *"What size shoe does your child wear?"* or *"How much does your child weigh?"* An informed or involved parent should know this information off the top of his or her head. If you are bad with numbers or are forgetful, you should review all such relevant data regarding your child before even considering sitting down for a deposition.

Finally, you may be asked open-ended or narrative questions. For example, "What kind of activities do you do with your child?" Now this sounds like a simple question, and perhaps it is. But remember, you are under oath and on the spot. A well thought out and thorough answer should be given. Answering "Everything" will not cut it, and the attorney will press you. Answering, "We play ball and go fishing," will likely be left alone and the attorney will move on because he will have what he wants...testimony that you *only* play ball and go fishing with your child. He will then refer you to that deposition question at trial when you try to tell the court how you ride bikes together, do homework, read stories, cook gourmet dinners, and go to church together. The courtroom questions will then likely sound something like this: *So were you lying then...or now? Did you just start doing these other activities? Had you forgotten all these things you do with your child on a regular basis...but now you remember?*

Therefore, preparing with your attorney prior to deposition is vital. Likewise, a little study and review of important facts is advisable as well. Finally, answer honestly and forthrightly in both deposition and trial.

Tips

1. When answering the discovery sent to you by the other attorney/party, do not be lazy. Be thorough, honest, and forthright.
2. The better job you do with your discovery answers will likely reduce attorney fees (your attorney will not have to spend additional time cleaning up your responses).
3. Notify your attorney early of any documents or information you want the other party to disclose so that they may modify their inquiries accordingly.
4. Prepare thoroughly for your deposition.
5. Maintain your demeanor throughout the process.

6

GUARDIANS AD LITEMS AND CUSTODY EVALUATORS: Who Is Looking Out for the Children?

During the course of your custody case, either attorney may petition the court for the appointment of a guardian ad litem or custody evaluator. Additionally, the court may on its own motion (*sua sponte*), appoint such a person. This person, within their particular disciplines, will investigate and report to the court a recommendation as to custody.

The Guardian Ad Litem

The guardian ad litem (GAL) is typically an attorney with additional training in the area of custodial determinations. He or she is appointed by the court—not the attorneys. He is a witness for the court and is often described as being "the eyes and ears of the court." The GAL will meet, at a minimum, with you, the other parent, and the child. He will review documents produced to him and listen to each parties' side of the story. He may also meet with your witnesses, conduct home visits, or investigate allegations on his own.

You should make every effort to comply with his requests and attempt to prove to him that you are the best parent for the job at hand. However, bear in mind that he is impartial with regards to the parties; it is his job to be on the side of the child and represent to the court what he believes is in the child's best interest. What is in the best interest of the child is not necessarily what is in your best interest. Finally, there is no attorney-client privilege as to your communications with this attorney. As stated consistently throughout this book, you should consult with your attorney throughout the process and seek his input before meeting with the GAL.

Typically, you should provide the GAL with as much evidence as he is willing to review. You should also make it a point to discuss the following:

- a brief personal history
- your involvement as a parent
- the needs of your child
- how you and the other parent either agree or diverge or disagree as to how best to provide
    o the education
    o the religious upbringing, and
    o the health care of your child
- any mental or physical health issues for yourself, the other parent or the children
- any criminal history for yourself or the other parent
- evidence as to the "status quo" of the child
- any evidence the other parent is not fit to be awarded custody
- visitation
- involvement of friends and family

After the GAL has completed his investigation, he will submit a written report to the court and your attorney based on your case facts as applied to the statutory concerns regarding the best interest of the minor child. You will be able to read and review this report before trial unless otherwise ordered by the judge. Under no circumstances should this document be provided to the children.

At trial, the GAL will listen to the trial testimony and then give a final report at the close of the trial. The parties' attorneys should be given the right to cross-examine the GAL on his recommendation.

The Custody Evaluator

Another method employed by the court to assist in making a determination as the best interest of the minor child is the appointment of a custody evaluator. Again, such a participant can be requested by either attorney via proper motion or on the motion of the court. The custody evaluator is typically a psychologist, psychiatrist, or similarly qualified individual with training to perform the necessary services for the court.

Like a GAL, she will meet with each party. However, instead of an investigation, she will conduct an evaluation. This evaluation usually consists of at least one interview and a series of psychological testing. Such tests typically include the **MMPI-2** (a test that professionals use to help measure psychopathology across a broad range of client settings), the **MCMI-II** (a self-report instrument designed to help the clinician assess DSM-IV-related personality disorders and clinical syndromes of a client), and the **QOLI (Quality of Life Inventory).** This test can help clinicians assess problems in living in sixteen areas of life for an individual and the degree to which the individual is satisfied or dissatisfied with each area in his or her own life, including health, self-esteem, goals and values, money, work, play, learning, creativity, helping, love, friends, children, relatives, home, neighborhood, and community.

Different evaluators may use additional or completely different assessment tests and tools. She may also interview or test the child, depending on the circumstances. By combining the test results and the information from her interviews with the party, she will make a recommendation to the court as to custody. These reports may be available to you or may be sealed due to the nature of the mental health information contained therein.

Upon review by the court and/or the attorneys, the custody evaluator may be brought into court to testify as to her findings, her recommendation and then cross-examined regarding said report.

Tips

1. The guardian ad litem and/or the custodial evaluator may be the most important witness in your case (excepting only yourself).
2. Cooperation with any appointed court witness/expert is vital.
3. The recommendation of such expert will carry a substantial amount of weight with the judge.
4. Any deficiencies that the GAL or evaluator may point out regarding your parenting should be addressed to the best of your abilities.
5. If you feel the GAL or evaluator is wrong or mistaken, in part or in total, consult your attorney before attempting to reconcile any such problems directly with the appointed expert.
6. Do not discuss the recommendation of a GAL or evaluator directly with the children unless advised to do so by competent counsel.

7

TRIAL PENDENCY:
What Is Happening Now?

So far, this book has attempted to explain certain facets of the custody case. We have discussed items to consider in anticipation of a trial and provided key points in your trial preparations. Additionally, we have discussed strategic and specific portions of your case that will be addressed during the pendency of your litigation. However, custody litigation is typically a long and arduous journey through the legal system. As such, this chapter will give you an overview of the overall legal process up to trial.

In a nutshell, the typical process is as follows:

1. Select your attorney
2. Gather your information
3. Determine your goals and strategy
4. File your case
5. Schedule status hearings
6. Filing or defending interim motions
7. Participate in mediation
8. Complete discovery
9. Appoint a guardian ad litem or custody evaluator
10. Attempt settlement negotiations
11. Prepare for the trial
12. Conduct the trial

Hiring an Attorney

Although it is legally permissible to represent yourself in a custody case, it is foolhardy at best. As stated throughout this book, nothing herein should be considered legal advice, nor is it intended as such. Applying your facts to your case and the applicable laws of your jurisdiction is the province and duty of your attorney. There is simply no substitute for a skilled and experienced attorney to guide you through a custody trial and ultimately present your case to the judge.

Gathering Your Information

After you have selected an attorney, he or she should request a comprehensive amount of information to assess your case. Typically, this information will be similar to that identified in Chapters 4 and 5 of this book. As each case varies, the attorney may request additional information for particular categories or in support of the unique facts of your case. On a practical note, the more thorough you are, the better understanding your attorney will have of the complexities of your case.

Determining Your Goals and Strategy

Once an attorney has sufficient information to assess your case, he will discuss your goals to help you determine a realistic course of action by either prosecuting or defending your case. If you have applied the information previously discussed in this book, you will have a head start on this process. However, your attorney will be able to discuss your goals more thoroughly and evaluate your chances of success.

So what do you want?

1. Custody
2. Visitation
3. Supervised or restricted visitation
4. Child support or reduced child support
5. A pound of flesh (vengeance)
6. Removal to another state or jurisdiction
7. Other issues

After you have outlined your goals and considered your chances of success, you can then begin creating a workable strategy. Be advised, you should not expect a top-secret plan, conspiracy, or the battle plans for a military-like mission. This strategy will consist of things such as when to file, when to attempt negotiations (if any), how to stress your strengths, how to exploit the other parent's weaknesses and how to overcome your own. Additionally, issues such as venue and jurisdiction, judge selection, discovery (as discussed in Chapter 5), expert witnesses and the employment of private investigators may also be considered in this strategy.

Filing Your Case

After you have a workable strategy, your case will be filed. This document is commonly referred to as a petition or complaint. The petition will then be served upon the other party by a law enforcement officer or duly licensed process server.

In the alternative, if you have been served with such a complaint, you will then have to file what is typically called a response or answer within a specific time. This time varies by jurisdiction throughout the United States; therefore, you should consult your state law and, of course, an attorney. Failure to respond in a timely fashion may result in a default order being entered against you (in other words—you lose).

Status Hearings

Most jurisdictions will assign a status date upon filing of the petition. This hearing is usually scheduled shortly after the date the responsive pleading is due for the initial pleading. This court setting allows the judge to review the file, verify if an answer has been timely filed, and determine if any immediate action needs to be taken by the court itself.

At such a hearing, a court order is typically entered resetting the matter for an additional or subsequent case management, status, or pre-trial hearing date. This allows the court to monitor the progress of the case and maintain the flow of the court docket.

It is not unusual to have multiple court settings during the pendency of your case to monitor such things as discovery compliance; appointment of a mediator, guardian ad litem, or custody evaluator; and to determine if the matter is ready for final trial. Your attorney should advise you as to whether or not your presence is necessary at any such court setting.

Interim Motions

From the date of initial filing until the date of the final trial, there are a number of motions and pleadings that may be filed and presented to the court. A complete list of such motions and pleadings is virtually impossible to provide here, but many of the common pleadings include temporary relief petitions, motions to enforce, contempt petitions, restraining orders/motions, and motions to modify.

Temporary Relief Petitions: These petitions are arguably the most common of all pleadings filed with the court during the pendency of a custody case. By filing such a document, your attorney is requesting a temporary solution to the issues pending before the court. Such relief requests can take the form of a temporary assignment of custody, a temporary visitation schedule, a temporary award of child support, the temporary exclusive possession of the residence (essentially evicting the other party from his or her home) or even monetary assistance from the other party. A party may ask the court for one, several, or all of such remedies. Additional remedies, not mentioned above, may also be sought, depending on your circumstances.

A hearing on the request for temporary relief will then be scheduled. This is typically an evidentiary hearing and as such, both testimony and evidence will be presented to the court so that an informed judicial decision can be made. The parties will then be obligated to follow the temporary order of the court until the final hearing, unless otherwise modified at a later date.

Motions to Modify: These motions are typically used to modify existing orders. Such an existing order could be a previous custody or visitation order that a party is now challenging. However, if this is an initial custody case, the parties will likely use this type of motion to modify a temporary order (as discussed above) that needs to be changed. On a practical note, these types of motions are not a "do over." The court will require sufficient cause and evidence to reconsider its temporary orders. As such, these motions are more appropriately applied to fixing issues that perhaps were not addressed as part of the existing order or modifying a particular portion of an order to better fit the circumstances. For example, visitation is denied on a temporary basis while a parent is being investigated for child abuse. Upon completion of the investigation exonerating the parent of the allegations, he or she may now be able to modify the order to allow for unrestricted visitation.

Motions to Enforce and for Contempt: These motions are distinct but complementary. The motion to enforce places an issue before the judge wherein a party is requesting that the other be ordered to affirmatively act. For example, the court may have entered an order wherein the parties are to enroll the minor child in counseling and cooperate with said counseling. If one of the parties refused to cooperate with the counselor, make appointments, have the child attend or some other derivative portion of the order, he or she may brought before the judge so that cooperation may be enforced.

In the alternative, a motion for contempt may be filed to bring an issue before the court wherein a party is willfully and contemptuously refusing to comply with a court order. Such motions are typical when one party or the other interferes with the other parties' visitation with the child. This proceeding alerts the judge as to the disregard and violation of his order. The judge may then find the violating party in contempt and then sanction, penalize, or even sentence that party to a period in jail.

With regards to these actions, it is best to avoid being on the receiving end of either.

Restraining Orders: These orders, and the accompanying motions, are typically protective in nature as to the party or the child. In the event you or your child is abused or endangered by the actions of the other parent, such relief can be sought virtually at any time. Careful consideration should be given when attempting to avail yourself of this type of relief. All too often, a party may attempt to "play dirty" and use these types of proceedings to gain an advantage. Obviously, improper use of protective orders will not set well with the judge and can be detrimental to your final outcome, despite any temporary advantage that may be gained. Consult your attorney and discuss the pros and cons of seeking protective orders as opposed to temporary relief petitions and orders.

Mediation

Mediation has now become commonplace in custody cases, whether or not joint parenting is currently in effect or even ultimately feasible. There are two primary forms of mediation. First, mediation is required in existing joint parenting arrangements as outlined in Chapter 1. As therein discussed, the parties are to mediate before taking an unresolved issue before the court. The second, and more applicable here, is that of mediation in an attempt to pre-empt trial in an initial custody case.

This form of mediation is usually court-ordered while the case is pending and an impartial mediator is appointed by the judge. The parties must then meet with the mediator and attempt to reach a mutually agreeable resolution. If such an agreement is reached, the parties' agreement will be formalized and approved by the judge. This agreement will then be incorporated into the final order. However, if no agreement can be reached, the matter will be brought for trial before the judge.

Settlement Negotiations

Settlement negotiations may be attempted at any juncture in the custody proceeding and are typically not admissible in a final trial. However, for purposes of this book, I am placing settlement negotiations at this point of the pre-trial progression. Therefore, assuming mediation has failed, discovery (as discussed in Chapter 5) has been completed, and a guardian ad litem/custody evaluator has been employed (as discussed in Chapter 6), this case is ripe for settlement negotiations.

You should now be in possession of all of your evidence and that of the other parent. You may also be aware of the recommendation of the GAL or custody evaluator (whether you agree or not) and understand its relevance to your chances of success. As such, you will now find yourself in position to negotiate an informed settlement and avoid the added costs and risks associated with trial.

A settlement conference may be had with both parties and their respective counsel present or the parties may negotiate solely through the attorneys. In any event, if a settlement can be reached, it will be formalized and made into an enforceable court order.

Trial Preparation

If at this time, no settlement can be reached, you and your attorney will have to prepare for the trial itself. Witnesses will be interviewed (or re-interviewed), evidence will be cataloged and made ready for entry into evidence, your testimony will be reviewed (not rehearsed) and your attorney will coordinate all aspects as discussed in this book to present your best case to the judge.

Tips

1. Choose your attorney wisely.
2. The cheapest attorney is rarely the best choice—you get what you pay for.
3. Failing to act is acting. You must not ignore a case that is filed against you.
4. Take action as is necessary to protect yourself and your child on a temporary basis, if applicable.
5. Obey any temporary orders in effect regarding your case.
6. Mediation may be your best chance at resolving your case in a way that is mutually agreeable to *both* parties.
7. Not all the evidence you gathered will be used in trial.

8

TRIAL:
What Will the Judge Decide?

As the date of your trial nears, it is very common to try to comprehend exactly what your trial will be like, and how it will be decided. Unfortunately, television shows and movies do a good job showing the exciting and engaging portions of a trial, but do a poor job of showing the actual court process.

A brief summary of a typical trial is as follows:

1. Opening statement (of each party)
2. Plaintiff's case and cross-examination by the defendant
3. Defendant's case and cross-examination by the plaintiff
4. Plaintiff's rebuttal
5. Defendant's sur-rebuttal
6. Closing argument (of each party)

Opening Statements are presented (unless waived) by each attorney and provide the court with a brief overview of the facts and a statement of the relief sought by a particular party.

The Plaintiff's Case: In almost every cause of action, the plaintiff presents his or her case first. Many people have the misconception that the plaintiff's position is the most advantageous. It is commonly believed that by presenting your case to the judge first, he will be most strongly influenced by your petition or believe you to be the most injured of the parties. However plausible this may seem, it is incorrect; the judge should weigh both parties' facts, arguments, and evidence and render a fair judgment regardless of which party is the plaintiff.

The plaintiff's case (case in chief) is presented by calling the appropriate witnesses, introducing his or her testimony, and admitting evidence into the record through said witnesses. The defendant's attorney will then be permitted the opportunity to cross-examine the witness and challenge the evidence being introduced. Either attorney may object as the situation warrants.

After the plaintiff's attorney has called all applicable witnesses, including the plaintiff, and introduced all pertinent and relevant evidence and exhibits, the case-in-chief will be complete and the plaintiff will "rest." In essence, the plaintiff's part of the trial will be finished and no new evidence will presented on the plaintiff's behalf thereafter.

The Defendant's Case: After the plaintiff rests, the defendant will then present his or her case-in-chief. Just like the plaintiff's case, the defendant's attorney will call witnesses, introduce evidence, and admit exhibits. The plaintiff's attorney will be allowed to cross-examine the witnesses and challenge the evidence being introduced. The defendant will then rest and no new evidence will be presented on the defendant's behalf thereafter. The defendant's attorney should take the opportunity (during the defendant's case-in-chief) to rebut or refute any evidence he can with regards to the plaintiff's case-in-chief.

Plaintiff's Rebuttal: After the defendant rests, the plaintiff may present rebuttal testimony and evidence. This will not be new or additional evidence and is limited to evidence that will contradict or rebut that which was presented by the defendant in his or her case-in-chief.

Defendant's Sur-Rebuttal: The court may, but is not necessarily required to, allow the defendant a sur-rebuttal. This will be a brief and limited opportunity for the defendant to rebut *only* that information which the plaintiff presented during the plaintiff's rebuttal.

Closing Arguments: After rebuttal is complete, the court will allow first the plaintiff's attorney, then the defendant's attorney to make a closing argument. During the closing, the attorney will sum up the case-in-chief, stress the positives about his or her client (as presented in the case-in-chief) and reinforce any negatives of the other party. Additionally, the attorney will likely make an argument for his client's position and restate the specifics of what his or her client is requesting from the court.

Preparing for Your Court Appearance

Preparing for your court appearance is much like studying for a final exam in high school or college. In an exam-like setting, you review your text, your class notes, homework, and any other information relevant to the course. Likewise, as you prepare for your appearance before the judge and the testimony you will be providing, you should read and review your divorce journal, review your pictures, notes, evidentiary documents and review the Comprehensive Custody Questionnaire so that you are well prepared for the questions to come. Further, your attorney should discuss what questions to expect, how to maintain your demeanor while on the stand and how to respond when an objection is raised.

Finally, do not overlook your actual "appearance" before the court (in other words, outward confidence, cleanliness, dress, hair care, and so on). The judge considers not only the facts but how they are presented in the court room. Your demeanor, your posture, your facial expressions, and your overall personal style can affect how the judge reacts to the information that is provided. This in turn can affect how the judge ascertains your overall veracity.

Presenting Your Case

No matter whether you are the plaintiff or defendant, whether you are called to testify in your case-in-chief or as an adverse witness by the other party, you will need to testify in the custody proceeding.

As discussed previously, other witnesses may be used to present your case, but you are usually your best witness. Therefore, we will be discussing your case generally, but with you as the primary witness. Although your case may be a complex divorce or a simple visitation case, we will briefly cover those areas most typical in a custody case, namely: custody, visitation, and child support.

Custody: In most cases, custody is the crux of the matter. The rest of your case is almost ancillary to this main issue. If you do not prevail on custody, the only remaining issues are how much visitation you will receive and how much child support you will pay. Therefore, it is incumbent upon you to present your case thoroughly and with sufficient evidentiary weight to prevail. A typical outline of the testimony to be presented is set forth below:

1. Setting forth your background: Your testimony will likely begin with the basics: your name, your occupation, residence and the like. This gives the judge information as to who you are. Additional information such as your education level, social/church involvement, alcohol use, medical condition, and important aspects of your personhood (both positive and negative) can be used to further elucidate the judge.

2. Demonstrating what kind of parent you are: After painting a clear picture of who you are; testimony will likely move toward what kind of parent you are. Your attorney will ask questions that evoke the information outlined in Chapter 3 of this book. You will need to provide a history of your involvement with your child, involvement by the other parent, discuss the needs of your child and how you are best suited to be named the primary caregiver or sole custodian of the child. During this part of your testimony, you will need to address the "best interest of the child" standards as set forth in the applicable state statute.

Ideally, you should cover most, if not all of the following through your testimony and that of your other witnesses:

As to your child:

- The child's age and, in some jurisdictions, gender
- The child's health, both mental and physical
- The child's relationship with siblings, if any

- The child's relationship with each parent
- The child's relationship with family and friends
- The child's routine (home, school, community, etc.)
- The preference of the child, if of a certain age or sufficient maturity (if such hearsay is admissible)
- Whether the child has been abused by a parent

As to each of the parents:

- The health of the parents, both mental and physical
- The behavior of the parents, both good and bad
- The lifestyle and routine of the parents
- The ability to provide for the child
- The proposed residence of the child (home, school, etc.)
- The parent who has in the past acted as primary caregiver
- The ability of proposed custodial parent to foster the relationship of the child and the proposed non-custodial parent
- The wishes of the parents

3. Entry of evidence: Throughout your testimony, you will likely be given specific exhibits to identify and discuss. These documents will include the items you gathered and prepared as discussed in Chapter 4, as well as documents you may have obtained through your discovery requests as discussed in Chapter 5. Your attorney will have sorted through these exhibits to find and use the most poignant and useful. Be advised, it is highly unlikely that all your documents will be presented to the court. Further, not all of the documents presented to the court will ultimately be entered into evidence. However, once an exhibit is admitted into evidence by the judge, it becomes part of the record and the judge will use it as part of his final determination and ruling.

4. Attacking the other party: Your attorney may interlace attacks on the other parent throughout your testimony as you compare and contrast yourself and the other parent; or he may make a concentrated effort at a specific point in your testimony. Such attacks need to be carefully considered for both probative value as well as the effect it may have on the judge's perception of your

character. Thus, your attorney's judgment will be important in how to portray the proper balance of such testimony and evidence.

When presenting this part of your case, the divorce journal and your notes on the "bad behavior" may prove highly significant. By giving specifics on behavior, such as visitation problems, parental alienation, and other difficulties—bolstered by exact dates and the particulars of each event— will strengthen your case and lend credence to your testimony.

Visitation: When you are fighting for custody, you are also fighting for visitation. As previously explained in Chapter 1 of this book, custody is primarily an issue as to decision-making authority. Thereafter, visitation (or the time you spend with your child) is determined. Typically, the parent who is named sole custodian or primary custodian is granted more visitation or custodial periods with the child than the other parent. It follows naturally—the custodial parent needs more interaction with the child to facilitate the decision-making process.

Therefore, you will present testimony outlining the schedule you desire and that which you desire for the other party. At a minimum, issues that should be addressed include:

1. <u>The needs of the child</u>. A child's school schedule, sports schedule, involvement with social and religious activities should be outlined. Additional considerations should be given to any special needs of the child.
2. <u>The schedules and limitations of the respective parents</u>. Each parent may have restraints on his or her schedule due to work demands, mental or physical issues, or general inability to foster the wellbeing of the child.
3. <u>Visitation problems and other bad behaviors</u>. During the pendency of the custody case (and even prior to that) either parent may have acted inappropriately, interfered with visitation, committed a crime or otherwise endangered or abused the child.
4. <u>The best interest of the child</u>. Ultimately, a visitation schedule for the parties should be outlined in your testimony that you believe is consistent with the best interest of the child.

Significant thought and consideration should be given to this schedule and it should include regular visitation, holidays, and a summer schedule. A sample schedule is included in Appendix A and B of this book.

Child Support: If you are requesting custody, you will likely be seeking child support from the other parent. Child support amounts are typically dictated by a formula set forth by state statute and vary throughout the United States. In any event, you will be either seeking to maximize your child support award or attempting to minimize your financial responsibility to the other party. As such your testimony will likely focus on the following:

1. The needs of the child. The needs of the child may include the lifestyle the child is accustomed to prior to this case, medical and physical needs, and other necessities that can only be met financially.
2. Your income and expenses. Typically, the needs of the child are of primary concern to the court. However, deviations may be sought if you are either in need of more financial assistance for the child (as the child support recipient); or are unable to meet the statutory child support requirements due to your own expenses compared to your overall income (as the child support contributor).
3. Any other factors applicable to your jurisdiction. As stated earlier, state child support statutes vary from jurisdiction to jurisdiction. Your attorney can apply any relevant factors to argue for maximizing or minimizing a child support award.

The Decision

The court, at the close of the trial, will either make a decision immediately and pronounce same to the parties or take the matter under "advisement." If the court gives an immediate decision, he will typically give an oral pronouncement of his findings and final judgment. This oral judgment will be followed by a written order detailing his pronouncement and this will be provided to each party.

On the other hand, if the judge takes the matter under advisement he will then, outside the presence of the parties and attorneys, review the testimony and evidence, apply the applicable law, and ultimately provide a written order of his finding and judgment to the parties.

Tips

1. Your trial will be substantially different from anything you have seen on television or in the movies.
2. Maintain your composure throughout the trial. Avoid outbursts, eye rolls, vulgar language, or other like behavior.
3. Dress to impress.
4. Show the proper respect to the court and the judge.
5. Review your entire case before trial. Quiz yourself on things such as your child's teacher's name, the child's clothing size, and other relevant information.
6. Ask your attorney to prepare you for trial.
7. If you do not know the answer to a question—say so. It is better to not know than to guess and be wrong.
8. Tell the truth. Lying under oath can subject you to charges of perjury.
9. Take a notebook/paper and write questions or information for your attorney to read as the trial progresses. Do not try to talk to him or her during the trial.
10. The trial will be exhausting. Get a good night's sleep before trial and avoid drugs or alcohol before and during trial – no cocktails at lunch.
11. Bring your documents with you to trial. You may be able to provide your attorney with a missing or misplaced document, if necessary.
12. Pay attention throughout the trial.

9

POST-TRIAL:
Now You Have Custody—
What Do You Do With It?

This chapter is designed with two goals in mind. The first is to provide you with the understanding of what a final order means to you (even if you have not yet obtained resolution), and the second is to shed some light on how you may proceed upon receiving that final order.

The best way to think about your final order is to consider it a new law created and drafted just for you, the other parent, and your child. Just as you must follow your state laws regarding things such as traffic laws, ordinances and the criminal code, you must now follow the court's order. Although violation of this order may not be a criminal offense, it may subject you to contempt proceedings that may eventually lead to incarceration. Therefore, when in doubt, follow your order.

If your order is silent as to certain issues or you are unsure as to how to apply the order to a certain set of circumstances, do not hesitate to contact your attorney for his advice and clarification. Ultimately, it may be necessary to return to court for such clarification or an amendment to the final order.

However, if you have just received a final judgment from the court, there are also other avenues of relief that may be available to you. Typically, your attorney can file motions after final judgment to clarify the order, request reconsideration, or even appeal the judgment. Be advised, such motions are time-sensitive and you should consult your attorney immediately upon receiving a final order.

Ultimately, as time passes, the parties' situations may change. Likewise, the needs of your child may also change. Therefore, you should conduct a periodic review of the custodial arrangement, visitation, and child support with your attorney to discuss if a return to court is warranted.

In conclusion, you may have a final custody order, your trial may be complete, but so long as your child is a minor or otherwise reliant upon you, your custody case will remain a very real and dynamic part of your life.

I wish you the very best of luck!

10

FREQUENTLY ASKED QUESTIONS

Q: **How long until the custody proceeding is over?**

A: It takes two people to agree, but only one to argue. As such, it depends on the parties. Thus, the sooner an agreement is reached, the sooner a final order can be entered. However, if no agreement can be reached, the matter will have to be decided by a judge. Depending on the court's availability, trial dates are usually set anywhere from one to six months out from the date the parties complete the pretrial discovery and motions. Typically you should expect a total time (from filing to trial) of six to eighteen months.

Q: **Does it matter if I am the plaintiff or the defendant?**

A: There is typically no *legal* benefit of being one or the other. Some parties find satisfaction in being the plaintiff—"the one to file"—but this is more of a psychological issue than a factual advantage. The plaintiff usually presents his or her case *first* to the judge (a primacy argument can be made) but then the defendant has the *last word* to the judge (a recency argument can therefore be made). A judge should be affected by neither.

Q: **Do I have to have an attorney?**

A: In a word—no. If you choose to proceed on your own—*pro se*—you may. However, as set forth in this book repeatedly, nothing herein should be considered as legal advice and this information should not be used as such. If you represent yourself, proceed with caution.

Q: **What if I am not the father?**

A: This is a loaded question and the answer depends upon your underlying goals. If you are not the father and want out of any perceived parentage, proper motions must be filed and proof (such as DNA tests) will likely be required. On the other hand, if you have acted as the father and wish to remain so, you may need to proceed with adoption proceedings to protect your relationship with the child. Without legal recognition of parentage, you may very well lack the standing to request visitation, effectively terminating your relationship permanently with the child.

Q: **Should I allow visitation without a court order?**

A: Without full knowledge of your situation, a simple answer (yes or no) cannot be given. This issue is typically the hot button in the beginning of any contested custody matter. Until an order is entered, married parents usually have "equal" right to the child. As such, either can take the child and then refuse to return the child to the other. However, this risk must be weighed against the perception of whether or not you are interfering with or failing to foster a relationship with the other parent. Thus, the complex answer is: yes, you *should* allow visitation, but not until you have considered the ramifications fully and assessed the facts of your situation. And, should the facts so indicate: no, you *should not* allow visitation.

Q: **Can I move away with my child?**

A: As discussed in Chapter 4, if you move, you should take the child with you if possible to maintain your position as custodian. However, there is a substantial difference between moving across town and across the state. Further, moving out of the state you live in is even more problematic and may violate state statutes. Therefore, any move should be discussed with your attorney first and careful consideration should be given as to how such a move will affect your case.

Q: Can I date while the case is pending?

A: In most states, dating will have no effect on the custody determination unless it negatively affects the child. However, anyone you date will likely become a witness. As a side note, if you are married, many states have laws prohibiting adultery or fornication that could come into play. Additionally, there is potential for civil action by your spouse against your paramour for interference with the marital union. As these laws and causes of action vary greatly from state to state, you should consult your attorney regarding dating—whether married or not—while your custody case is pending.

Q: What if my child does not want to go to/back to the other parent?

A: As discussed in Chapter 9, the court order is substantially a "law" for you, the other parent and your child. As such, it must be followed. Allowing your child to decide as to whether or not he or she will "follow the law" sets a bad example and I believe teaches the child a disregard for authority. Further, it may subject you to civil contempt or even criminal charges for visitation interference. And it will be YOU that is charged—not your child. However, if there is health or safety reasons to consider, you must put your child's welfare first. Consult your attorney as soon as possible if this issue arises.

Q: Can I make the other parent testify in court?

A: Yes, you can call the other parent to testify in your case. In fact, it is often advisable to do so to elicit certain testimony that will not likely be voluntarily disclosed by that person. Calling the other party as an adverse witness or hostile witness is a trial tactic that you should discuss with your attorney as part of your trial preparation. Further, you should be prepared to be called by the other attorney for the same reasons.

Q: I have an existing custody order, how can I change it?

A: Changing or modifying an existing order is substantially the same as the initial proceeding. The information in this book can be used in a modification trial as well as in the initial proceeding. The only difference is the current status quo has been established by the order and modification of that status must meet the statutory considerations for modification as outlined by your state laws.

APPENDICES

APPENDIX A

JOINT PARENTING AGREEMENT

IN THE CIRCUIT COURT
FOR THE TWENTIETH JUDICIAL CIRCUIT
ST. CLAIR COUNTY, ILLINOIS

ROSE SMITH,	)
	)
Petitioner,	)
	) No.: <u>12-D-123</u>
vs.	)
	)
RICHARD SMITH,	)
	)
Respondent.	)

<u>JOINT PARENTING AGREEMENT</u>

The following is submitted to the court by agreement of the Plaintiff, Rose Smith hereafter referred to as "Mother" and Defendant, Richard Smith, hereafter referred to as "Father", as a proposed plan for the sharing of custodial and child care responsibilities pursuant to, and in compliance with the purposes of the Illinois Marriage and Dissolution of Marriage Act as set forth in Section 102 thereof and in accordance with the procedures set forth in Section 602 of that Act. The parties agree to the following terms of this plan, which is to be incorporated in a subsequent Judgment for Dissolution of Marriage, the terms are as follows:

1. JOINT CUSTODY. It is acknowledged that both parties are fit and proper persons to have the joint legal care, custody, control, and education of the minor children of the parties, namely:

Children's Names	Ages
Date of Birth	
John Smith	8
10/22/2002	
Susan Smith	5
12/13/2004	

The parties further agree that they shall have the joint legal custody of the children but that the permanent physical care, custody, control, and place of principal residence for the children shall be with the Mother.

We further agree that joint parenting is best facilitated by close proximity of both parents to the children so as to maximize the children's time with both parents. Therefore, we agree that Rose Smith shall not change the primary and legal residence from the _____ school district unless the parties agree in writing. Any request for change shall be decided in accordance with the following provisions relating to dispute resolutions set forth below.

2. ACCESS TO MEDICAL RECORDS AND SCHOOL INFORMATION. Both parties shall participate actively in raising and guiding the children. To that end, the parties shall share all information in connection with medical, dental, and psychological needs as well as the children's education and progress in school. Both parties shall sign the necessary forms for Medical and School records for the children and such records shall be made available to both parents. Each parent shall be notified of consultations and invited to confer with teachers, counselors, or medical professionals concerning education and health care.

3. EMERGENCIES AND MEDICATIONS. In case of emergency, where time does not allow consultation with the other parent, the parent with the physical custody (possession) of the children shall take whatever emergency action is necessary to meet the health care or other need. As soon as possible thereafter, the parent making such an emergency decision will advise the other parent of the same. We agree to inform each other of any medical or health problems which may have arisen while either has had custody of the children. We shall provide each other with any medications which the children is taking at the time of transfer of custody and with sufficient information to allow the parent assuming physical custody to obtain refills of that medication.

4. JOINT DECISIONS. Both parents acknowledge that in matters of major concern, including but not limited to education, religious training, extraordinary medical care, and extracurricular activities, the parties will consult with each other and make every effort to reach vital decisions jointly. As the physical custodian, the Mother shall apprize the Father of the necessity of making such a vital decision, and the Father shall do likewise when the need for a decision arises while the children are in his physical possession. In the event the parties do not agree as to a decision regarding areas of major concern, the parties shall submit their dispute to mediation as set forth in paragraph 13 below.

5. REMOVAL OF CHILDREN FROM THE STATE OF ILLINOIS. The parties agree that neither parent will permanently remove the residence of the children from the State of Illinois without the written agreement of the other parent or permission of the court based on the best interest and welfare of the children.

6. VISITATION. The Father shall have visitation rights with the child as the parties agree but, at a minimum, shall include the following:

A. WEEKLY AND WEEKEND VISITATION: The Father shall have visitation every Wednesday from 5:00 p.m. until 9:00 a.m. (or at the beginning of school) on Thursday and on alternate weekends from 5:00 p.m. on Friday until 5:00 p.m. Sunday beginning the 1st weekend after the entry of the Dissolution of Marriage.

B. LEGAL OR SCHOOL HOLIDAYS: The Parties will also receive the following visitation on legal or school holidays where the children attend or reside beginning at 9:00 a.m. and ending at 6:00 p.m.(or unless otherwise specified). In the event that a party is exercising weekend visitation and a holiday as set

forth below is on a Friday or Monday immediately before or
after said weekend, the parent exercising custody/visitation shall
be entitled to keep the children overnight between the holiday
and weekend period.

The Father shall have the following schedule:

Even Numbered Years		Odd Numbered Years
New Year's Day		Martin Luther King's Birthday
Good Friday		President's Day
Memorial Day		Independence Day- 9am to 9am on July 5th
Labor Day		Columbus Day
Veterans' Day		Thanksgiving Day
Christmas Day		Halloween - 9am to 9pm

The Mother shall have the following schedule:

Odd Numbered Years		Even Numbered Years
New Year's Day		Martin Luther King's Birthday
Good Friday		President's Day
Memorial Day		Independence Day- 9am to 9am on July 5th

Odd Numbered Years		Even Numbered Years
Labor Day		Columbus Day
Veterans' Day		Thanksgiving Day
Christmas Day		Halloween 9am to 9pm

C. VACATIONS: The parties will also receive the following visitation during summer vacation, winter vacation (or Christmas break), spring break (or Easter break) as herein specified:

1. Summer Vacation:

    The Father will receive two (2) consecutive weeks of vacation during the summer as celebrated in the schools in the community where the child resides or attends not to interfere with any holidays set forth in Paragraph B above. Visitation shall begin at 6:00 p.m. on the selected Friday and ending on the second succeeding Friday at 6:00 p.m. The Father shall provide no less than thirty (30) days advance notice of his selected weeks.

    The Mother will receive two (2) consecutive weeks each summer vacation as celebrated in the schools in the community where the child resides or attends not to interfere with any holidays set forth in Paragraph B above. Visitation shall begin at 6:00 p.m. on the selected Friday and ending on the second succeeding Friday at 6:00 p.m. The Mother shall provide no less than thirty (30) days advance notice of her selected weeks.

    The Mother's selected weeks shall have precedence in Odd numbered years and the Father's selected weeks shall have precedence in Even numbered years. Each parent shall begin his or her summer vacation periods on his/her regularly scheduled weekend as set forth in "A" above.

2. Winter or Christmas Vacation:

The Father shall have visitation Even-numbered years beginning 8:00 a.m. on the first scheduled day of vacation as celebrated in the schools in the community where the child resides or attends and ending December 26 at 7:00 p.m. On odd-numbered years, beginning at 7:00 p.m. December 26 and ending at 8:00 p.m. on the following New Year's Day.

The Mother shall have visitation Odd-numbered years beginning 8:00 a.m. on the first scheduled day of vacation as celebrated in the schools in the community where the child resides or attends and ending December 26 at 7:00 p.m. On Even-numbered years, beginning at 7:00 p.m. December 26 and ending at 8:00 p.m. on the following New Year's Day.

3. Spring or Easter Vacation:

The Father shall have visitation on Even-numbered years beginning at 8:00 a.m. of the first full day of said vacation as celebrated in the schools in the community where the children reside or attends and ending at 9:00 p.m. on the evening before said vacation ends.

The Mother shall have visitation on Odd-numbered years beginning at 8:00 a.m. of the first full day of said vacation as celebrated in the schools in the community where the children reside or attends and ending at 9:00 p.m. on the evening before said vacation ends.

D. MISCELLANEOUS: The Father will also be entitled to the following miscellaneous visitation periods:

1. Father's Day of every year from 8:00 a.m. to 9:00 p.m.;
2. Father's birthday every year from 8:00 a.m. to 9:00 p.m.;
3. Child's birthday during even-numbered years from 8:00 a.m. to 9:00 p.m., but only during such hours of that child's birthday that such child is not otherwise attending school or some function thereof.

The Mother will be entitled to retain physical custody of the minor children, irrespective of any provision to the contrary herein, during the following periods:

1. Mother's Day of every year from 8:00 a.m. to 9:00 p.m.;
2. Mother's birthday every year from 8:00 a.m. to 9:00 p.m.;
3. Child's birthday during odd-numbered years from 8:00 a.m. to 9:00 p.m.

If any of the specific days set forth in B, C, and D of this paragraph conflict with the visitation set forth in A of this paragraph, then the specific provisions set forth in B, C, and D shall be controlling. Additionally, in the event a visitation period is made unavailable by virtue of serious illness or injury of the children, the parties shall cooperate to implement a reasonable substitute visitation period, bearing in mind the best interest of the children.

7. MODIFICATION OF VISITATION BY AGREEMENT. The parties, by written agreement, shall have the right to alter, modify, and otherwise arrange for specific visitation periods other than those shown above and on such terms and conditions as are conducive to the best interests and welfare of the children.

8. TRANSPORTATION.

The Father shall pick up the children at the beginning time for all his physical custody (visitation).

The Mother shall pick up the children at the beginning time for all her physical custody (visitation).

9. PARENTAL NOTICE. Each parent agrees to keep the other informed as to the exact place where each of them resides, the phone numbers of their homes and places of employment, and if either parent travels out-of-town for any period of more than (3) days then such person shall notify the other of his or her destination and shall maintain a cell phone number where he or she can be reached.

10. CHILD ENDANGERMENT PROHIBITION. Both parents agree that at all times when the children are under their physical care, each shall refrain from placing the children in an environment or exposing the children to activities that may endanger the children's physical, mental, emotional or moral well-being. Both parents agree to avoid controlled substances or excessive use of alcoholic beverages or prescription medication when the minor children are in their physical custody.

11. ADDITIONAL PROVISIONS. The parties shall adhere to the following rules with respect to the custody of and visitation with the minor children;

a. Each parent shall refrain from discussing the conduct of the other parent in the presence of the children except in a laudatory or complimentary way;

b. Under no circumstances shall the question of child support, either as to amount, manner or transmission of payment, be raised in the presence of the children;

c. Visitation with the minor children shall not be withheld because of the non-payment of child support. The payment of child support shall not be withheld because of the refusal of the Principal Residential Custodian to grant visitation to the Non-Principal Residential Custodian;

d. The Principal Residential Custodian shall not threaten to withhold visitation from the Non-Principal Residential Custodian. The Non-Principal Residential Custodian shall not threaten to prevent or delay the return of the children to the Principal Residential Custodian after a period of visitation;

e. The Principal Residential Custodian shall prepare the children both physically and mentally for visitation with the Non-

Principal Residential Custodian. The children shall be available at the time mutually agreed upon between the parties for the beginning of visitation;

f. The Non-Principal Residential Custodian shall advise the Principal Residential Custodian as soon as possible if the Non-Principal Residential Custodian is unable to keep a planned visitation with the children;

g. Neither parent shall unreasonably question the children regarding the activities of the other parent;

h. The Non-Principal Residential Custodian shall not visit the children at unreasonable hours;

i. The Non-Principal Residential Custodian shall work with the Principal Residential Custodian to arrange visitation schedules which shall take into account the children's education, athletic and social activities. The Non-Principal Residential Custodian may take the children to appropriately planned activities;

12. SCHOOL INFORMATION AND ACTIVITIES. The parties shall jointly determine where the children shall be enrolled in school and take the necessary action with the school authorities of the schools in which the children are to be enrolled to:

a. List the Non-Principal Residential Custodian as a parent of the children;

b. Authorize the school to release to the Non-Principal Residential Custodian any and all information concerning the children;

c. Insure that the Non-Principal Residential Custodian receives copies of any notices regarding the children.

d. The Principal Residential Custodian shall promptly transmit to the Non-Principal Residential Custodian any information received concerning parent-teacher meetings, school club meetings, school programs, athletic schedules and any other school activities in which the children may be engaged or interested within 14 days of receipt.

e. The Principal Residential Custodian shall promptly, after receipt of same, furnish to the Non-Principal Residential Custodian a photocopy of the children's grade or report card and copies of any other reports concerning the children's status or progress.

f. The Principal Residential Custodian shall, when possible, arrange appointments for parent-teacher conferences at a time when the Non-Principal Residential Custodian can be present and whenever possible they shall be attended by both parents.

13. DISPUTE RESOLUTION, CHANGE OF CIRCUMSTANCE, AND PERIODIC REVIEW. The parents acknowledge that they are attempting to resolve their differences through-the use of this joint parenting agreement and they recognize that the details herein may require future adjustments and changes to reflect the children's best interest.

The parents also recognize that this joint parenting agreement is a dynamic concept subject to re-evaluation and change based upon a substantial change in circumstances of a parent or child. To determine whether different arrangements might better suit future circumstances, the parents hereby agree and stipulate:

a. This agreement shall be reviewed jointly by us at least on an annual basis;

b. That in the event the parents cannot agree as to a vital non-emergency decision affecting the welfare of the children the Circuit Court of _____ County shall retain continuing jurisdiction to adjudicate any disputed issue. The parties agree, however, that if any conflicts arise between the parents as to any of the provisions of this Joint Parenting Agreement or the implementation thereof, that the complaining parent shall first notify the other parent of the nature of the complaint and both parents shall make reasonable attempts to negotiate a settlement of the conflict.

Wherever practicable under the circumstances complaints shall be made in writing and given to or mailed to the other parent. Complaints shall include suggestions for resolutions to the issues raised. The parent receiving the complaint shall respond in writing. The response shall indicate what issues are agreed to and make suggestions for resolution of the remaining issues.

If the parties are unable to resolve their conflict within a reasonable period of time the parties must submit any such disputed issue or conflict for resolution to an impartial mediator, mutually agreed upon, before applying to the Court for relief as to all matters which do not involve serious endangerment of the children's physical, mental, moral or emotional health. In the event the parties cannot agree as to the mediator, or if the mediation is unsuccessful, or if an immediate and serious endangerment is alleged, a court proceeding may be filed by either party.

If the parties choose an impartial mediator they shall attempt to agree to the proportions each shall pay for the mediation services. If the mediation is unsuccessful, the cost of the mediator may be included in a petition for fees and costs in connection with the court proceeding.

c. Until the conflict is resolved (either by agreement or judicial ruling) the parent exercising physical custody shall continue to make such day-to-day decisions as may be necessary to protect the best interests of the children, but shall take no action with reference to the area in dispute which would prejudice or take unfair advantage of the other party.

The parties hereto, on behalf of their minor children, respectfully submit the foregoing Joint Parenting Agreement for this Court's approval and incorporation in the Judgment for Dissolution of Marriage to be entered herein.

_____

Richard Smith

_____

Rose Smith

STAN R. WELLER
The Weller Law Firm
120 West Main Street
Suite 212
Belleville, IL 62220
(618)277-3476

APPENDIX B

SOLE PARENTING AGREEMENT

IN THE CIRCUIT COURT
FOR THE TWENTIETH JUDICIAL CIRCUIT
ST. CLAIR COUNTY, ILLINOIS

ROSE SMITH,	)	
	)	
Petitioner,	)	
	)	No.: 12-D-123
vs.	)	
	)	
RICHARD SMITH,	)	
	)	
Respondent.	)	

SOLE PARENTING AGREEMENT

The following is submitted to the court by agreement of the Petitioner, Richard Smith, hereafter referred to as "Father" and the Respondent, Rose Smith, hereafter referred to as "Mother", as a proposed plan for the sharing of child care responsibilities pursuant to the purposes of the Illinois Marriage and Dissolution of Marriage Act as set forth in Section 102 thereof and in accordance with the procedures set forth in Section 602 of that Act. The parties' agree to the following terms of the proposed plan, which will be incorporated in a subsequent Judgment for Dissolution of Marriage, the terms are as follows:

1. SOLE CUSTODY. It is acknowledged that the Mother is the fit and proper person to have the primary residence, care, custody, control, and education of the minor child of the parties, namely:

Children's Names	Ages
Date of Birth	
John Smith	8
10/22/2002	
Susan Smith	5
12/13/2004	

The parties therefore agree that the Mother shall have sole legal custody of the child and that the permanent physical care, custody, control, and place of principal residence for the child shall be with the Mother.

2. ACCESS TO MEDICAL RECORDS AND INFORMATION. Both parties shall participate actively in raising and guiding the child and to that end shall share all information in connection with medical, dental, and psychological needs as well as the child(ren)'s education and progress in school. Both parties agree to sign the necessary forms for Medical and school records for the child(ren) and such records shall be made available to both parents, and each of them shall be notified of consultations and invited to confer with teachers, counselors, or medical professionals concerning education and health care. However, any final decision regarding the above shall rest solely with the Mother.

3. EMERGENCIES AND MEDICATIONS. In case of emergency, where time does not allow consultation with the other parent, the parent with the physical care of the child(ren)'s shall take whatever emergency action is necessary to meet the health care or other need. As soon as possible thereafter, the parent making such an emergency decision will advise the other parent of the same. We agree to inform each other of any medical or health problems which may have arisen while either of us has care of the child(ren). We shall provide each other with any medications which the child(ren) is(are) taking at the time of transfer of possession of the minor child(ren) and with sufficient information to allow the parent assuming physical care to obtain refills of that medication. However, any final decision regarding the above shall rest solely with the Mother.

4. REMOVAL OF CHILD FROM THE STATE OF ILLINOIS. The parties agree that neither parent will permanently remove the residence of the child from the State of Illinois without the written agreement of the other parent or permission of the court based on the best interest and welfare of the child.

5. VISITATION. The Father shall have visitation rights with the child, which currently shall include the following:

A. WEEKLY AND WEEKEND VISITATION: The Father shall have visitation every Wednesday from 5:00 p.m. to 9:00 a.m. (or at the beginning of school) and on alternate weekends from 5:00 p.m. on Friday until 5:00 p.m. Sunday beginning the 1st weekend after the entry of the Dissolution of Marriage.

B. LEGAL OR SCHOOL HOLIDAYS: The Parties will also receive the following visitation on legal or school holidays beginning at 9:00 a.m. and ending   at 6:00 p.m. (or unless otherwise specified). In the event that a party is exercising weekend visitation and a holiday as set forth below is on a Friday or Monday immediately before or after said weekend, the parent exercising custody/visitation shall be entitled to keep the children overnight between the holiday and weekend period.

The Father shall have the following schedule:

Even Numbered Years	Odd Numbered Years
New Year's Day	Martin Luther King's Birthday
Good Friday	President's Day
Memorial Day	Independence Day- 9am to 9am on July 5th
Labor Day	Columbus Day

Even Numbered Years		Odd Numbered Years
Veterans' Day		Thanksgiving Day
Christmas Day		Halloween - 9am to 9pm

The Mother shall have the following schedule:

Odd Numbered Years		Even Numbered Years
New Year's Day		Martin Luther King's Birthday
Good Friday		President's Day
Memorial Day		Independence Day- 9am to 9am on July 5th
Labor Day		Columbus Day
Veterans' Day		Thanksgiving Day
Christmas Day		Halloween 9am to 9pm

C. VACATIONS: The parties will also receive the following visitation during summer vacation, winter vacation (or Christmas break), spring break (or Easter break) as herein specified:

    1. Summer Vacation:

        The Father will receive two (2) consecutive weeks of vacation during the summer as celebrated in the schools in the community where the child resides or attends not to interfere with any holidays set forth in Paragraph B above. Visitation shall begin at 6:00 p.m. on the selected Friday and ending on the second succeeding Friday at 6:00 p.m. The Father shall provide no less than thirty (30) days advance notice of his selected weeks.

The Mother will receive two (2) consecutive weeks each summer vacation as celebrated in the schools in the community where the child resides or attends not to interfere with any holidays set forth in Paragraph B above. Visitation shall begin at 6:00 p.m. on the selected Friday and ending on the second succeeding Friday at 6:00 p.m. The Mother shall provide no less than thirty (30) days advance notice of her selected weeks.

The Mother's selected weeks shall have precedence in Odd numbered years and the Father's selected weeks shall have precedence in Even numbered years. Each parent shall begin his or her summer vacation periods on his/her regularly scheduled weekend as set forth in "A" above.

2. Winter or Christmas Vacation:

The Father shall have visitation Even-numbered years beginning 8:00 a.m. on the first scheduled day of vacation as celebrated in the schools in the community where the child resides and ending December 26 at 7:00 p.m. On odd-numbered years, beginning at 7:00 p.m. December 26 and ending at 8:00 p.m. on the following New Year's Day.

The Mother shall have visitation Odd-numbered years beginning 8:00 a.m. on the first scheduled day of vacation as celebrated in the schools in the community where the child resides and ending December 26 at 7:00 p.m. On Even-numbered years, beginning at 7:00 p.m. December 26 and ending at 8:00 p.m. on the following New Year's Day.

3. Spring or Easter Vacation:

The Father shall have visitation on Even-numbered years beginning at 8:00 a.m. of the first full day of said vacation as celebrated in the schools in the community where the children reside and ending at 9:00 p.m. on the evening before said vacation ends.

The Mother shall have visitation on Odd-numbered years beginning at 8:00 a.m. of the first full day of said vacation as celebrated in the schools in the community where the children reside and ending at 9:00 p.m. on the evening before said vacation ends.

D. MISCELLANEOUS: The Father will also be entitled to the following miscellaneous visitation periods:

1. Father's Day of every year from 8:00 a.m. to 9:00 p.m.;
2. Father's birthday every year from 8:00 a.m. to 9:00 p.m.;
3. Child's birthday during even-numbered years from 8:00 a.m. to 9:00 p.m., but only during such hours of that child's birthday that such child is not otherwise attending school or some function thereof.

The Mother will be entitled to retain physical custody of the minor children, irrespective of any provision to the contrary herein, during the following periods:

1. Mother's Day of every year from 8:00 a.m. to 9:00 p.m.;
2. Mother's birthday every year from 8:00 a.m. to 9:00 p.m.;
3. Child's birthday during odd-numbered years from 8:00 a.m. to 9:00 p.m.

If any of the specific days set forth in B, C, and D of this paragraph conflict with the visitation set forth in A of this paragraph, then the specific provisions set forth in B, C, and D shall be controlling.

6. MODIFICATION OF VISITATION BY AGREEMENT. The parties, by written agreement, shall have the right to alter, modify, and otherwise arrange for specific visitation periods other than those shown above and on such terms and conditions as are conducive to the best interests and welfare of the child. In the event a visitation period is made unavailable by virtue of serious illness or injury of the child, the parties shall cooperate to implement a reasonable substitute visitation period, bearing in mind the best interest of the child.

7. TRANSPORTATION. The Father shall pick up the child at the beginning time for all visitation. The Father shall drop off the child at the termination of all visitation.

8. PARENTAL NOTICE. Each parent agrees to keep the other informed as to the exact place where each of them resides, the phone numbers of their homes and places of employment, and if either parent travels out-of-town, with the child, for any period of more than (3) days then such person shall notify the other of his or her destination and shall maintain a cell phone where he or she can be reached.

9. CHILD ENDANGERMENT PROHIBITION. Both parents agree that at all times when the child are under their physical care, each shall refrain from placing the child in an environment or exposing the child to activities that may endanger the child's physical, mental, emotional or moral well-being. Both parents agree to avoid controlled substances or excessive use of alcoholic beverages or prescription medication when the minor child is in their physical custody.

The parties hereto, on behalf of their minor child, respectfully submit the foregoing Parenting Agreement for this court's approval and incorporation in the Judgment for Dissolution of Marriage to be entered herein.

_____
Petitioner

_____
Respondent

APPENDIX C

BEST INTEREST OF THE CHILD SAMPLE STATUTES

Illinois: 750 ILCS 5/602

§ 602. Best Interest of Child.

(a) The court shall determine custody in accordance with the best interest of the child. The court shall consider all relevant factors including:

(1) the wishes of the child's parent or parents as to his custody;

(2) the wishes of the child as to his custodian;

(3) the interaction and interrelationship of the child with his parent or parents, his siblings and any other person who may significantly affect the child's best interest;

(4) the child's adjustment to his home, school and community;

(5) the mental and physical health of all individuals involved;

(6) the physical violence or threat of physical violence by the child's potential custodian, whether directed against the child or directed against another person;

(7) the occurrence of ongoing or repeated abuse as defined in Section 103 of the Illinois Domestic Violence Act of 1986, [FN1] whether directed against the child or directed against another person;

(8) the willingness and ability of each parent to facilitate and encourage a close and continuing relationship between the other parent and the child;

(9) whether one of the parents is a sex offender; and

(10) the terms of a parent's military family-care plan that a parent must complete before deployment if a parent is a member of the United States Armed Forces who is being deployed.

In the case of a custody proceeding in which a stepparent has standing under Section 601, it is presumed to be in the best interest of the minor child that the natural parent have the custody of the minor child unless the presumption is rebutted by the stepparent.

(b) The court shall not consider conduct of a present or proposed custodian that does not affect his relationship to the child.

(c) Unless the court finds the occurrence of ongoing abuse as defined in Section 103 of the Illinois Domestic Violence Act of 1986, the court shall presume that the maximum involvement and cooperation of both parents regarding the physical, mental, moral, and emotional well-being of their child is in the best interest of the child. There shall be no presumption in favor of or against joint custody.

CREDIT(S)

P.A. 80-923, § 602, eff. Oct. 1, 1977. Amended by P.A. 81-419, § 1, eff. Sept. 6, 1979; P.A. 84-795, § 1, eff. Jan. 1, 1986; P.A. 85-1417, § 1, eff. Jan. 1, 1989; P.A. 86-612, § 1, eff. Jan. 1, 1990; P.A. 87-1186, § 2, eff. Jan. 1, 1993; P.A. 88-409, § 1, eff. Aug. 20, 1993; P.A. 90-782, § 5, eff. Aug. 14, 1998; P.A. 94-377, § 5, eff. July 29, 2005; P.A. 94-643, § 5, eff. Jan. 1, 2006; P.A. 95-331, § 1125, eff. Aug. 21, 2007; P.A. 96-676, § 5, eff. Jan. 1, 2010.

Formerly Ill.Rev.Stat.1991, ch. 40, ¶ 602.

[FN1] 750 ILCS 60/103.

Current through P.A. 97-679 of the 2011 Reg. Sess.

Tennessee: T. C. A. § 36-6-106

36-6-106. Child custody.

(a) In a suit for annulment, divorce, separate maintenance, or in any other proceeding requiring the court to make a custody determination regarding a minor child, the determination shall be made on the basis of the best interest of the child. In taking into account the child's best interest, the court shall order a custody arrangement that permits both parents to enjoy the maximum participation possible in the life of the child consistent with the factors set out in subdivisions (a)(1)-(10), the location of the residences of the parents, the child's need for stability and all other relevant factors. The court shall consider all relevant factors, including the following, where applicable:

(1) The love, affection and emotional ties existing between the parents or caregivers and the child;

(2) The disposition of the parents or caregivers to provide the child with food, clothing, medical care, education and other necessary care and the degree to which a parent or caregiver has been the primary caregiver;

(3) The importance of continuity in the child's life and the length of time the child has lived in a stable, satisfactory environment; provided, that, where there is a finding, under subdivision (a)(8), of child abuse, as defined in § 39-15-401 or § 39-15-402, or child sexual abuse, as defined in § 37-1-602, by one (1) parent, and that a nonperpetrating parent or caregiver has relocated in order to flee the perpetrating parent, that the relocation shall not weigh against an award of custody;

(4) The stability of the family unit of the parents or caregivers;

(5) The mental and physical health of the parents or caregivers;

(6) The home, school and community record of the child;

(7)(A) The reasonable preference of the child, if twelve (12) years of age or older;

(B) The court may hear the preference of a younger child on request. The preferences of older children should normally be given greater weight than those of younger children;

(8) Evidence of physical or emotional abuse to the child, to the other parent or to any other person; provided, that, where there are allegations that one (1) parent has committed child abuse, as defined in § 39-15-401 or § 39-15-402, or child sexual abuse, as defined in § 37-1-602, against a family member, the court shall consider all evidence relevant to the physical and emotional safety of the child, and determine, by a clear preponderance of the evidence, whether such abuse has occurred. The court shall include in its decision a written finding of all evidence, and all findings of facts connected to the evidence. In addition, the court shall, where appropriate, refer any issues of abuse to the juvenile court for further proceedings;

(9) The character and behavior of any other person who resides in or frequents the home of a parent or caregiver and the person's interactions with the child; and

(10) Each parent's or caregiver's past and potential for future performance of parenting responsibilities, including the willingness and ability of each of the parents and caregivers to facilitate and encourage a close and continuing parent-child relationship between the child and both of the child's parents, consistent with the best interest of the child.

(b) Notwithstanding the provisions of any law to the contrary, the court has jurisdiction to make an initial custody determination regarding a minor child or may modify a prior order of child custody upon finding that the custodial parent has been convicted of or found civilly liable for the intentional and wrongful death of the child's other parent or legal guardian.

(c) As used in this section, "caregiver" has the meaning ascribed to that term in § 37-5-501.

(d) Nothing in subsections (a) and (c) shall be construed to affect or diminish the constitutional rights of parents that may arise during and are inherent in custody proceedings.

CREDIT(S)

1995 Pub.Acts, c. 428, § 2, eff. June 12, 1995; 1998 Pub.Acts, c. 1003, § 1, eff. May 18, 1998; 1998 Pub.Acts, c. 1095, §§ 2, 3, eff. July 1, 1998; 2000 Pub.Acts, c. 683, § 2, eff. May 8, 2000; 2007 Pub.Acts, c. 245, §§ 1 to 3, eff. May 24, 2007; 2011 Pub.Acts, c. 433, § 1, eff. June 6, 2011.

Current through end of 2011 First Reg. Sess.

Arizona: A.R.S. § 25-403

§ 25-403. Custody; best interests of child

A. The court shall determine custody, either originally or on petition for modification, in accordance with the best interests of the child. The court shall consider all relevant factors, including:

1. The wishes of the child's parent or parents as to custody.

2. The wishes of the child as to the custodian.

3. The interaction and interrelationship of the child with the child's parent or parents, the child's siblings and any other person who may significantly affect the child's best interest.

4. The child's adjustment to home, school and community.

5. The mental and physical health of all individuals involved.

6. Which parent is more likely to allow the child frequent and meaningful continuing contact with the other parent. This paragraph does not apply if the court determines that a parent is acting in good faith to protect the child from witnessing an act of domestic violence or being a victim of domestic violence or child abuse.

7. Whether one parent, both parents or neither parent has provided primary care of the child.

8. The nature and extent of coercion or duress used by a parent in obtaining an agreement regarding custody.

9. Whether a parent has complied with chapter 3, article 5 of this title. [FN1]

10. Whether either parent was convicted of an act of false reporting of child abuse or neglect under § 13-2907.02.

11. Whether there has been domestic violence or child abuse as defined in § 25-403.03.

B. In a contested custody case, the court shall make specific findings on the record about all relevant factors and the reasons for which the decision is in the best interests of the child.

CREDIT(S)

Added by Laws 2005, Ch. 45, § 4. Amended by Laws 2009, Ch. 57, § 1.

[FN1] Section 25-351 et seq.

Current through the end of the Fiftieth Legislature, First Regular Session and Fourth Special Session (2011), and also includes election results from the November 2, 2010 general election

APPENDIX D

COMPREHENSIVE CUSTODY QUESTIONNAIRE

Enter the percentage of involvement each of you have had regarding the indicated tasks and activities:

Infant/Toddler Care

Activity/Responsibility	% Mother	% Father
Feeding	_____	_____
Diaper changes	_____	_____
Holding/comforting	_____	_____
Bathing	_____	_____
Brushing teeth	_____	_____
Dressing	_____	_____
Put to bed	_____	_____
Reading stories	_____	_____
Discipline	_____	_____

Explain: _____
Other: Examples: _____

Health Care

Activity/Responsibility	% Mother	% Father
Doctor visits	_____	_____
Dental visits	_____	_____
Orthodontist visits	_____	_____
Taking care of child when sick	_____	_____

Other: Examples: _____

Daily Care

Activity/Responsibility	% Mother	% Father
Preparing meals	_____	_____
Grocery shopping	_____	_____
Laundry	_____	_____

Clothes shopping   _____   _____

Shopping for school supplies   _____   _____

Arranging childcard/daycare   _____   _____

Taking to/picking up from daycare   _____   _____

Teaching values   _____   _____

Teaching manners   _____   _____

Assignment of child's chores   _____   _____
(or enforcement)

Playing indoors   _____   _____
        Examples: _____

Playing outdoors   _____   _____
        Examples: _____

Cleaning home

Other: Examples: _____   _____   _____

School Years

Activity/Responsibility	% Mother	% Father
Bathing		
Styling hair	_____	_____
Hair cuts	_____	_____
Preparing lunches	_____	_____
Dressing	_____	_____
Brushing teeth (help or reminding)	_____	_____
Bedtime enforcement	_____	_____
Reading stories, books	_____	_____
Helping with homework	_____	_____
Taking to/picking up from school	_____	_____
Taking to/picking up from extracurricular activities	_____	_____
Teacher's conferences	_____	_____
Attending open houses	_____	_____
School volunteering	_____	_____
Attending PTA/PTO meetings	_____	_____
Examples: _____	_____	_____
Discipline		
Explain: _____	_____	_____
Other: Examples: _____		

Extracurricular Activities

Activity/Responsibility	% Mother	% Father
Taking to/picking up from church/activities	_____	_____
Taking to/picking up from sports activities	_____	_____
Coaching	_____	_____
Taking to/picking up from lessons	_____	_____
Hosting birthday parties	_____	_____
Other: Examples: _____		

Answer each of the following:

Describe your typical daily and weekly schedule, including work schedule:

> Include: Travel away from home, "on call" times, and any other applicable concerns.

Describe the other parents typical daily and weekly schedule, including work schedule:

> Include: Travel away from home, "on call" times, and any other applicable concerns.

Describe your typical day as it relates to your child:

- Has this schedule been different in the past? If so, how?

List the school where the child(ren) attend, the grade, teacher and years attended at that school.

- List previous schools and the reason for any changes:

List each residence where you or the child has resided since the child's birth.

List all potential witnesses who have spent significant time in your home, with you or your child, or significant time with your child.

List any visitation problems you have experienced. Explain.

List any incidents of parental alienation or other incidents wherein the other party has attempted to poison the mind of your child against you.

List any crimes: felony, misdemeanor or traffic in which you or the other parent has been convicted.

List any reasons why you believe the other parent is unfit.

List any evidence or incidents of abuse against you or your child by the other parent. Include dates and any other relevant facts.

List any behaviors, activities or other habits of the other parent that may endanger your child.

List any behaviors, activities or other habits that may negatively affect the morals or ethics of your child.

List any mental health concerns you have about the other parent or any that he or she may allege against you.

List all sports, extracurricular activities or hobbies your child is engaged in and your involvement is each.

List all relatives for you and the other parent who are involved with the children (even marginally) and describe said involvement.

List any other significant issues you wish to address.

APPENDIX E

DIVORCE JOURNAL

<u>HIS</u>

1/10/12   MOM took kids to School
            I picked them up from school, helped with their
            homework and put them to bed (kids at my house
            tonight)

1/11/12   Dropped kids off at school
            MOM picked up kids (kids at her house tonight)
            Called kids at 7:00 p.m. NO ANSWER – left message
            Called kids at 9:00 p.m. NO ANSWER

1/12/12   No contact with MOM or kids today

1/13/12   Picked kids up at school for my weekend
            Kids said they heard me on the machine but MOM said
            "don't answer"
            Made homemade pizzas with the kids and rented the
            movie *UP* and watched with kids
            No call from MOM

1/14/12   Took kids to soccer game and watched
            Took kids out to dinner
            Played video games with kids 'til bed time
            MOM called at 3:00 p.m., talked to each child

1/15/12   Took kids to Church
            Grandma and Grandpa came to house for fried chicken
            dinner. They stayed until MOM picked kids up at 5:30
            p.m. (she was 30 minutes late and did not call)

DIVORCE JOURNAL

<u>HERS</u>

1/10/12   DAD took kids to School
               I picked them up from school, helped with their
               homework and put them to bed (kids at my house
               tonight)

1/11/12   Dropped kids off at school
               DAD picked up kids (kids at his house tonight)
               Called kids at 7:00 p.m. NO ANSWER – left message
               Called kids at 9:00 p.m. NO ANSWER

1/12/12   No contact with DAD or kids today

1/13/12   Picked kids up at school for my weekend
               Kids said they heard me on the machine but DAD said
               "don't answer"
               Made homemade pizzas with the kids and rented the
               movie *UP* and watched with kids
               No call from DAD

1/14/12   Took kids to soccer game and watched
               Took kids out to dinner
               Played video games with kids 'til bed time
               DAD called at 3:00 p.m. talked to each child

1/15/12   Took kids to Church
               Grandma and Grandpa came to house for fried chicken
               dinner. They stayed until DAD picked kids up at 5:30
               p.m. (he was 30 minutes late and did not call)

ABOUT THE AUTHOR

Attorney Stan R. Weller is a sole practitioner in the Southern Illinois/Metro East St. Louis area. He established The Weller Law Firm in 2006 after many years in private firms as well as a period with the Illinois Attorney General's Office working in the Sexually Violent Persons Unit. He received his Bachelor of Science from the University of Wisconsin Madison in 1992 and his Juris Doctorate from the Southern Illinois University in Carbondale in 1998. He is a certified mediator, arbitrator, and former guardian ad litem, but concentrates his practice in the areas of family law and bankruptcy.

Mr. Weller is a founding member of BASIL (Bankruptcy Attorneys of Southern Illinois) and has been a featured speaker at the annual BASIL conference. He is also a member of the Illinois State Bar Association and numerous other legal and professional organizations.

Mr. Weller was a contributing author of the *Inside the Minds* book, *Understanding the Effects of BAPCPA: Leading Lawyers on Examining BAPCPA Changes, Adopting New Filing Strategies, and Analyzing Consumer Bankruptcy Trends*; and is the author of the family law book, *Marital Settlement and Joint Parenting Agreements Line by Line: A Detailed Look at Marital Settlement and Joint Parenting Agreements and How to Draft Them to Meet Your Clients' Needs.*

ASPATORE

ABOUT THE AUTHOR

Attorney Stan R. Weller is a sole practitioner in the Southern Illinois/Metro East St. Louis area. He established The Weller Law Firm in 2006 after many years in private firms as well as a period with the Illinois Attorney General's Office working in the Sexually Violent Persons Unit. He received his Bachelor of Science from the University of Wisconsin Madison in 1992 and his Juris Doctorate from the Southern Illinois University in Carbondale in 1998. He is a certified mediator, arbitrator, and former guardian ad litem, but concentrates his practice in the areas of family law and bankruptcy.

Mr. Weller is a founding member of BASIL (Bankruptcy Attorneys of Southern Illinois) and has been a featured speaker at the annual BASIL conference. He is also a member of the Illinois State Bar Association and numerous other legal and professional organizations.

Mr. Weller was a contributing author of the *Inside the Minds* book, *Understanding the Effects of BAPCPA: Leading Lawyers on Examining BAPCPA Changes, Adopting New Filing Strategies, and Analyzing Consumer Bankruptcy Trends*; and is the author of the family law book, *Marital Settlement and Joint Parenting Agreements Line by Line: A Detailed Look at Marital Settlement and Joint Parenting Agreements and How to Draft Them to Meet Your Clients' Needs.*

ASPATORE